Winter Fun in
Northern California
& Nevada

Bear Klaw Press
Environmental Guide Series

Winter Fun in Northern California & Nevada

A Guide to *All* the Major Trailheads
for
Snowshoeing, Nordic Skiing, Snowmobiling
and
Alpine Skiing, Snowboarding, Skating, Sledding and Snowplay Areas

Including a Personal, Driving, and Sports Winter Safety Manual

Bern Kreissman

Bear Klaw Press
Davis, California

Copyright © 1997 Bern Kreissman

Library of Congress Card Number: 96-086489
International Standard Book Number: 0-9627489-7-8

Typing of manuscript by Kathy Huntziker, Pages Plus.

Graphic design, typography, page layout production, and various
illustrations by Jeanne Pietrzak and Jennifer Tomich, Graphic Gold.

Various illustrations and original cover design by Sue Wilkerson, Your
Next Design.

Final cover by Laurie Gigette Gould, Falcon Press Publishing.

Illustrations have been adapted from the following sources: CorelDraw® and
MasterClips® image packages; USDA Forest Service, Pacific Northwest Region;
USDA Forest Service, Intermountain Region; USDA Forest Service, U.S. Ski
Association Tahoe Nordic Search and Rescue Team; Sacramento Bee research;
California Department of Boating and Waterways; Washington State Parks and
Recreation Commission.

Index by Teresa L. Jacobsen.

Manufactured in the United States of America
10 9 8 7 6 5 4 3 2 1

Library of Congress Cataloging in Publication Data
Kreissman, Bern
Winter Fun in Northern California & Nevada
Includes index

Bear Klaw Press
926 Plum Lane, Davis, California 95616
Phone: 916-753-7788, Fax: 916-753-7788

Dedicated to the Past

Sonia and Nathan
Eva and Morris

You may be a little cold on some nights, on mountain tops above the timber-line, but you will see the stars.

—John Muir

❄ Contents

❄

❄❄ Introduction

Snowshoeing, Nordic skiing, snowboarding, and snowmobiling are the fastest growing winter sports in the nation, and nowhere can they be enjoyed on a wider range than in California. Nine great national parks, 19 national forests and numerous state parks grace California. Four of the national parks and all of the forests offer winter recreation areas or facilities. All of the forests offer snowshoe and Nordic ski trails, 13 hold alpine ski resorts, and 14 provide snowmobile areas.

The number of possible trailheads is limitless, for any snowed-over road (except where restrictions may be in force) is a snowmobile and snowshoe trailhead, and every safe parking niche on any of the mountain roads which permit parking is a potential starting point for Nordic skiers or snowshoers. In the Mendocino National Forest, for instance, there are no formal trailheads, but at the higher elevations, Forest Service Road 7 leads to snowshoe and cross country ski areas, snow play sites, and even some snowmobiling. Similar starting points may be made on every unplowed county road and multi-acre public woodland tract in the state.

It would be folly to attempt, and impossible to achieve, a guide to all such trailheads. Nonetheless, this work lists every trailhead and area which has been specifically designated for recreation by a public agency such as a national forest ranger district, or a private entity such as a ski resort. In some very few instances, an extremely popular area outside of such designation has also been included. These listings, thus, include almost 100 percent of the groomed or marked snow trails of California and Nevada.

The directory which follows the safety manual is divided into four sections: 1) Snowshoe and Nordic Ski Trailheads, 2) Snowmobile Trailheads, 3) Alpine Ski Resorts, (including snowboarding) and, 4) Snowplay Areas. In only rare instances are snowshoers banned from Nordic ski trails. In the vast majority of cases, snowshoers and cross-country skiers share the same trails (though snowshoers may be requested to keep clear of the ski track itself). Therefore, snowshoe and Nordic ski starting sites are presented together. Consequently, a reference to either sport refers equally to both. Similarly, snowboarders are now welcomed at most Alpine resorts, and unless specifically noted to the contrary, all references to downhill ski areas include snowboarding. Snowmobile areas, however, are listed separately. In most instances snowmobile trails are open to snowshoers and skiers, though the reverse is seldom true. The snowplay section lists areas for sledding and tubing, tobogganing, sleighing, dog-sledding, snowman building, and other snow amusements. It will also show ice skating rinks and outdoor sites. Many commercial winter sports areas operate within a national forest by special use permit from the Forest Service.

The information in the directory shows:
• The full name and administrative unit of the area. Commercial area administrative units are synonymous with their names.
• Road directions to the trailhead, resort, or site.
• A brief description of the area.
• Fee or no fee. Where fees are applied, the charge may

vary according to the day of the week, the season, holiday periods, the size of the group, the age of the participants, or other factors. To be certain of potential costs, call before the start of your trip. Sno-Park fees as of January 1997 are $3.00 for a one day pass and $20.00 dollars for a season pass (November 1 through May 30). Oregon and Washington Sno-Park permits are honored in California, and your California permit is honored in those states.

• Telephone numbers for further information.

These listings are followed by a second directory showing the addresses of all the public agencies noted in this work. Finally, the index by Teresa Jacobsen will permit readers to find, expeditiously, any particular trailhead.

The introductory safety manual is abstracted, and in several instances taken directly, from a variety of government publications, particularly those of the California Department of Transportation, the California Department of Parks and Recreation, and the Forest Service. "Forest Service" is abbreviated to FS throughout the work.

This work would not have been possible without the unreserved cooperation of every recreation officer in every national forest ranger district in the state. To each of them and to their colleagues, I send my deepest thanks. Special thanks go to Connie Finster and Bryan Klock of the California Department of Parks and Recreation Sno-Park Program who gave generously of their time and expertise.

My thanks also to Jeannette Crowley, Mike Hall, Robert Hammond, Ken Karkula, Scott Lanioreux, Jon M. Silvius, and, especially Jean M. Hawthorne of the Forest Service for their expert advice. A very special note of gratitude to Karen Finlayson of the Eldorado National

Forest Information Center and her colleague for their counsel and their engaging spirit and warm good humor.

The author would be pleased to receive additional or corrected information for a contemplated second edition. Your correspondence is invited. Letters should be addressed to the author in care of Bear Klaw Press.

Bern Kreissman
Davis, California 1997

Section I ❄

Winter Safety

Each winter, newspapers, radio, and television carry grisly reports of fatal car accidents on iced-over roads, of lost skiers found frozen a stone's throw from warmth and security, of snowshoers overwhelmed and devastated by avalanches they themselves had triggered, and of outdoor revelers in flimsy party clothing suddenly overtaken and ravaged by fierce winter gales. Many of these obituary accounts carry an underlying note of how easily the dreadful denouement might have been avoided if only the victims had prepared properly. Play in the snow can be a glorious adventure, but winter conditions are always afoot to remind us that tragedy is lying in wait for the uncaring, the unwary, the unprepared.

1 ❄
Winter Driving

Driving in winter's cold, wet, snowy, and icy conditions challenges your car engine to the fullest. To meet such circumstances, your car should be at maximum operating efficiency. Before venturing into snow country, you should make a thorough check of the electrical system (battery, ignition, and lights), brakes, tires, exhaust, heating and cooling systems, and windshield wipers and washers. Be sure your car is winterized.

- Check your antifreeze and be prepared for colder temperatures.
- Make sure your windshield washer reservoir is full. You may wish to add a special solvent to prevent icing.
- Create a winter driving kit for the car:
  - Tire chains, repair links, and tighteners
  - Ice scraper
  - Small broom or stiff brush to remove snow from roof, hood, and headlights. Snow left on any of these areas increases the potential for decreased visibility when the car is put in motion.
  - Large rag or old towel to wipe slush and snow from the lights and mirrors.
  - Paper towels
  - Kitty litter (or sand) for added traction under the drive wheels.
  - Traction mats
  - Snow shovel

– Blanket, emergency blanket, and extra warm clothes.
– Plastic garbage bags and/or tarpaulin to lie on when applying chains.
– Flashlight and extra batteries
– First aid kit (especially for scraped knuckles after you have applied the chains.)
– Battery jumper cables
– Tow cable
– Candle lantern
– Portable AM/FM radio and extra battery
– Extra food and water.
– Flares

Chain Controls

Always carry ch.ains, chain tighteners and repair links. A ground sheet to keep you dry while installing the chains is a convenience. You must stop and install chains when highway signs indicate that chains are required. You will be cited by the Highway Patrol if you do not comply. Normally, the checkpoint is approximately a mile beyond the first "chains required" signs. Be aware that control areas may move rapidly from one point to another because of changing weather or road conditions. When chains are required, wait until you can pull off the highway to the right completely and safely. Do not stop in a traffic lane; you will put yourself in great danger. Be sure to apply the chains to the drive wheels of your car.

The speed limit is almost always 25 miles an hour when chains are required, but may be posted higher, to 40 miles per hour, if the conditions warrant a higher speed. The appropriate limit will be posted along the highway. Driving at a higher speed invites a traffic citation and chain and car damage to boot.

If you use the services of a chain installer, be sure to get a receipt and make a note of the installer's badge number in case of later difficulties. The installer is an independent entrepreneur, not a state employee. Installers are not allowed to sell or rent chains. When removing chains, pull well beyond the signs reading "end chain control" to an uncongested pull-off area to the right, where you may remove them safely. Avoid those areas where many cars obstruct the highway.

Road Delays and Closures

Weather and road conditions can change rapidly and may occasion a change in chain control points or a closure of the highway. A highway that was open when you drove up may be closed or be under chain restrictions when you start down. Accidents or spinouts, which may block the road for hours, happen frequently during storms. Routes Interstate 80 and U.S. 50, because of heavy traffic, are particularly vulnerable to accidents and consequent closure. Zero or very low visibility caused by blowing snow in high winds also call for roadway closure. Such closures occur frequently on I-80 during winter storms.

In an effort to reduce storm accident rates on I-80, the highway department meters eastbound traffic (permits fewer cars and sets a time delay between cars) at Applegate, nine miles east of Auburn. Similarly, traffic on highway U.S. 50 may be metered at Pollock Pines and Meyers. Westbound traffic is metered, similarly, at the Nevada state line. Metering not only results in fewer accidents, it also reduces congestion at the chain-on areas. Waiting at Applegate, below the severe weather area, is far more pleasant than sitting out a storm on the highway, and it also allows drivers the option of returning home or passing the time in a warm restaurant.

Driving in Snow

The most important element in winter driving is mind-set. Drivers must be aware constantly of road conditions and the traffic about them, and they must drive at speeds appropriate to the weather, road condition, visibility, and traffic. Drivers should be snugly dressed and comfortably seated, and bulky, heavy clothes and gloves should be removed at the first safe opportunity to stop (never struggle out of a coat or a sweater while the car is in motion). Lightweight, non-constricting, warm outerwear, which allows drivers to concentrate on driving, is recommended. A full zipper jacket, a light warm hat, and thin leather gloves are ideal for winter motoring.

Drivers should be seated comfortably in easy reach of the foot pedals, with seat and shoulder belts in place. Easy-on, easy-off sunglasses are a must for winter driving.

Before setting the car in gear, start the engine and turn the heat control to "hot" for two minutes before switching on the defrost button. Preheating will prevent moisture from fogging the inside of the windshield when warm air hits the glass. If the windshield or windows do fog up, open a window a crack, and turn the defroster fan to maximum. Be sure your wipers are off before you start your engine to protect the blades and the wiper motor.

To start a car on ice or snow, make sure there is a clear path for the wheels for several feet—some shoveling may be necessary. Ease out of the parking space without spinning the drive wheels. Keep your front wheels straight and maintain a low speed at a low gear (second or reverse depending on your parking situation). You may need traction assistance with a traction mat, kitty litter, or sand under the drive wheels. If you use such aids, be sure no one is standing in a direct line with the drive wheels. Many a bystander has been hurt by objects thrown up by the drive wheels. Gently rocking the car back and forth with no wheel spinning may allow you to get out of an iced-over patch of the parking lot. Never gun the motor if you get stuck; spinning wheels will only dig you deeper into the hole. You must use minimum power to keep the wheels from spinning. Many car manuals recommend procedures for rocking a car out of a bad patch.

Always allow extra time for a trip in or out of snow country. Winter trips to the mountains are consistently more time consuming than similar trips in dry weather so allow for such added time in your travel plans.

Keep your gas tank as full as possible. One cannot predict serious traffic delays or major detours caused by weather, road closures, or accidents. Try to keep your tank at least half-full to avoid gas line freeze up.

Keep your windshields and windows clear. Stop at a safe turnout to brush snow and slush from the glass areas and mirrors.

Slow down. Drive at speeds appropriate to the prevailing conditions. Stopping distances are much greater on ice and snow than on dry surfaces, as much as eight times longer, so keep at least twelve car lengths back of the vehicle before you. Keep your speed low and steady, do not accelerate quickly, and avoid unnecessary turns or lane changes. Try to maintain a straight course. On approaching a hill take note of other drivers' actions, and stay far enough behind the car immediately ahead so that you may avoid a slowdown or a stop. Sufficient space in front of your car will allow you to maneuver carefully, avoid any stranded vehicle, and change speeds if necessary to carry the car over the crest. On the downhill, use low gear to slow down and stay off the brakes as much as possible to avoid skids. If braking, pump the brakes lightly (but not on a car with anti-lock brakes!); gentle, slow brake applications (squeeze braking) are recommended by AAA to avoid locking the wheels and skidding.

If you start to skid, do not panic and do not hit the brakes! Turn the front wheels in the direction the rear of the car is skidding. Then easily turn the wheel in the opposite direction to straighten out.

Stopping on ice requires particular care. AAA recommends squeeze braking with de-clutching (manual transmission) or shifting to neutral (automatic transmission) along with the "heel and toe" method. "Keep the heel of your foot on the floor and use only your toes to apply firm, steady pressure on the brake pedal just short of lockup, the point at which the wheels stop turning." You must keep your heel on the floor! With anti-lock brakes on the other hand, "do not pump the pedal or remove your foot from the brake."

AAA also recommends that you not use your parking brake in snow country. Slush can freeze all parts of the brake system and lock the emergency brake. Automatic shift cars should be left with the shift arm in "Park" position, and manual transmission vehicles should park in first gear or reverse. If advisable, chock your wheels. The Automobile Association advises drivers to be sure their "fender wells and exhaust pipes are clear of ice and snow" since frozen slush can trap the front wheels and make steering impossible, and plugged exhaust pipes are dangerous.

Driving in Fog

Since fog is a frequent accompanist of winter weather, special precautions should be taken when driving in reduced visibility circumstances:
- Slow down
- To change lanes or cross traffic, roll down the window to listen for cars you may not be able to see
- Keep your low beam headlights on. Remember to turn them off when parking.

- Keep your windshield clear
- If you must stop, pull off the highway as far as possible and step away from your car to a safe zone

Driving in Rain

Driving in a hard rain also limits visibility and driving precautions as for fog prevail. In a teeming downpour it is smart to stop at a rest area or a protected road zone to wait out the deluge. If you must stop on the highway, pull off the roadway as far as possible. Also remember that the first ten minutes of a heavy storm are the most dangerous as rainfall mixes with road-oil and debris to form a slick surface. If the car is stuck in mud, follow all the rules for starting on ice.

Be aware of the potential for hydroplaning—a situation in which the tires lose contact with the road, often resulting in skids. Keep your tires properly inflated and watch for possible hydroplaning circumstances—standing water, rain drops bubbling on the road, or sloshing noises from the tires. At thirty miles per hour, properly inflated tires with good tread will maintain contact with the road. Cars traveling at sixty miles per hour may hydroplane regardless of the merit of the tires. To reduce the chances of hydroplaning, slow down, avoid hard braking or sharp turning, drive in the tracks of the vehicle ahead, and increase the distance to the car immediately ahead of you to at least twelve car lengths. Slow down in any case; a mid-size car on a wet road driving at 60 miles per hour needs 280 feet to come to a stop. At 75 miles per hour, 545 feet is required—that's almost two football fields.

California Highway Information Network

Caltrans provides telephone information updated every two hours for the 16,000 miles of highway in the state. During the winter months, driving conditions are featured, as well as notices of road closures, one-way controlled traffic, construction work areas, and other traffic descriptions. Driving conditions requiring chains are sometimes given in code:

R1: Chains required except for autos and trucks with snow tires.

R2: Chains required on all vehicles except four-wheel drive cars with snow tires on all four wheels.

R3: Chains required on all vehicles with no exceptions.

R1 and R2 are the most common conditions. The highway is usually closed before an R3 condition is imposed.

To access the network within California, call 1-800-427-7623 (ROAD) from a touch-tone phone. The touch-tone system allows you to enter the highway route number(s), such as "5," "101," "99," "80," "50," or "49" to receive late breaking road condition information for any highway(s) you plan to travel. Dial phone users may call (916) 445-1534 for recorded information on a small number of major roadways. Dial service is unlikely to transmit useful information, so one should use a touch-tone instrument if at all possible.

California Highway Information Broadcast Network

Caltrans also operates the California Highway Information Broadcast Network (CHIBN), a wire service to subscribing radio and television stations, updated at least hourly. Road conditions may be heard on the following stations.

Sacramento/San Joaquin Valley Area
KFBK/KGBY 1530 AM/92.5 FM—Sacramento
KRAK 1140 AM/105.1 FM—Sacramento

KOVR TV, Channel 13—Sacramento
KPAY 1060 AM/95.1 FM—Chico
KALF 95.7 FM—Chico
KCEZ 100.7 FM—Chico
KBLF 1490 AM/95.7 FM—Red Bluff
KHOP 104.1 FM—Modesto
KAAT 107.1 FM—Oakhurst
KWAC 1490 AM—Bakersfield

San Francisco Bay/North Coastal Area
KGO 810 AM—San Francisco
KRED 1480 AM/92.3 FM—Eureka
KFLI/KEKA 790 AM/101.5 FM—Eureka
KATA/KFMI 1340 AM/96.3 FM—Arcata
KMUD 91.1 FM—Garberville
KLLK 1250 AM—Willits
KWNE 93.5 FM/94.5 FM—Ukiah

Sierra Nevada Area
KAHI/KHYL 950 AM/101.1 FM—Auburn/Sacramento
KTHO 590 AM/102.9 FM—South Lake Tahoe
KOWL/KRLT 1490 AM/93.9 FM—South Lake Tahoe
KROW/KNEV 780 AM/95.5 FM—Reno
KKBN 93.5 FM—Twain Harte
KVML/KZSQ 1450 AM/92.7 FM—Sonora
KMMT 106.3 FM—Mammoth Lakes
KIBS/KBOV 1230 AM/100.7 FM—Bishop
KPTL/KKGL 1300 AM/102.9 FM—Carson City

Northern Area
KCNO 570 AM/94.5 FM—Alturas
KNCQ 97.3 FM—Redding
KRCR TV, Channel 7—Redding
KSYC/KYRE 1490 AM/97.7 FM—Yreka
KSUE 1240 AM/93.3 FM—Susanville
KPCO 1370 AM—Quincy

Thirdly, Caltrans operates Caltrans Radio during storms. The department broadcasts road condition information on low frequency radio transmitters along some mountain highways. Watch for road signs along the way and turn your radio to the frequency given. Transmission range is generally two to three miles. There are six permanent installations on I-80 between Vacaville and Truckee. On U.S. 50, Caltrans has one transmitter near Pollock Pines. Portable transmitters are also used when conditions warrant.

Information Sources

In addition to Caltrans' services, information may be received for a variety of other winter activities.

- Avalanche information for Lake Tahoe and the eastern Sierra is available from the Forest Service at (916) 587-2158.

- Road, weather, and avalanche condition news for Yosemite is attainable from the National Park Service at (209) 372-0200.

- Sierra Nevada weather and forecasts are provided by the Sacramento Municipal Utilities District (SMUD) at (916) 646-2000.

- Weather conditions for Lake Tahoe, Reno and Routes 80 and 50 are broadcast from the Sierra Weather Network at 1-800-988-8225.

- Tahoe weather and road conditions (as well as entertainment, food, and accommodations) may be heard on the Lake Tahoe Hotline, (916) 546-5253 from North Shore Lake Tahoe, (916) 542-4636 from South Shore Lake Tahoe, and (702) 831-6677 from Reno, Sparks, and Carson City.

Safety Recommendations

Before you go, check road and weather conditions, and be sure that your car and gear are equal to a worst possible scenario situation. Leave word with a responsible party:

- Where you are going—leave a marked map
- When you plan to depart
- When you plan to return
- Who you are going with

Eat before you start your snowshoe or Nordic ski trip, and nibble frequently during the outing. Eat before you get hungry, drink before you get thirsty. Drink plentifully throughout the day (no alcoholic beverages). Do not eat snow. Melting snow in your mouth saps energy and cools your body core.

2 ❄
Clothing for Snowshoers, Nordic Skiers, Snow Campers

The layering system for clothing provides the greatest comfort and warmth with the lightest weight and the fewest garments. With three lightweight layers, a contemporary snowshoer can be warmer and more comfortable than the nineteenth century fur-trapper in a twenty-pound bear-skin coat and a five-pound beaver hat. Multiple layers allow snowshoers, Nordic skiers, hikers, or any strenuous winter sports enthusiasts to adjust their attire easily in response to changes in weather and, particularly, body temperature. As snowshoers and Nordic skiers know, body heat fluctuates markedly as they tramp uphill, stop for lunch, run into a rain or snow squall, reach windy peaks, or glissade downhill in deep shade.

Base Layer

Since your body will pump out anywhere from two to four quarts of perspiration on a strenuous trek, the primary function of the base layer is to transport the sweat away from the body; it should also provide warmth.

Underwear and Socks: Synthetic long underwear and lightweight synthetic socks do the job best. Wool is acceptable since it will keep you warm when wet, but it can be heavy, soggy, and itchy, and it is more expensive than synthetics. Treated polyester, polypropylene and the score of associated variants are the fabrics of choice for the base layer. Cotton, when wet with perspiration, will draw the heat from your body and can kill you. Never, never, never wear cotton underwear.

Synthetic longjohns and shirts generally come in three weights: light, medium, or expedition weight. Wear the weight suitable for the weather conditions and the exertion level of the activity. Light or medium suits are generally best during active periods of an outing. Expedition weight serves best on winter camping excursions or on longer stretches of inactivity. Insulated underwear is not a good idea unless you are planning to sit still in the wilderness for lengthy junctures (ice fishing, sleigh riding). Generally, insulated underwear will not transport perspiration effectively, and it prevents the possibility of an easy cool-down when overheated. Thus, it destroys the adaptability of attire required by active outdoor sportspeople.

Gloves: Soft polypropylene glove liners as the first layer on the hands provide the versatility all snow trekkers need—easy adaptability from no protection, to light protection, to full protection.

Insulating Layer

Socks: Over the soft synthetic sock next to the foot, wear a heavy cushioning outersock. Currently, any wool, bulky synthetic, or wool synthetic blends are among the most popular outersocks. Rising fast in acceptance, particularly for winter sports enthusiasts, are the flatseamed fleece socks, such as those made of Polartec 300 by Acorn Products Co. (Lewiston, Maine). These relatively new socks are remarkably warm, breathable, moisture-managing, odor resistant, and easy to care for. Polartec seems sure to vie with, and possibly eclipse, wool as the sock fabric of choice in the future.

Another sure bet for future popularity are the waterproof-breathable socks made with a laminate or film such as Gore-Tex. Dupont's "Seal Skinz" may be worn singly as a waterproof outer layer, or the insulated model may be worn as both an insulator and waterproofer. As soon as prices fall to a reasonable range, one may expect to see most snowshoers in lightweight running shoes and waterproof breathable socks.

Boots: Nordic ski boots are required for cross-country skiers, but snowshoers have a choice—a conflicting choice—lightweight or waterproof. Since weight on the foot is onerous in hiking (a common truism holds that one pound on the foot is equal to 5-10 pounds on the back) and even more so in snowshoeing, a snowshoer should opt for the lightest possible boot consistent with day-long comfort. Snowshoers out for a lengthy day trip, and snow campers, should choose waterproof boots—particularly snow campers, since wet boots can ice over during the night. Recreational snowshoers may opt for dry feet with waterproof boots (or waterproof socks), neoprene over-the-shoe booties, or even lightweight rubbers. Avid snowshoe racers eschew even the over-shoe-booties and make their races in the lightest possible supportive canvas, or leather running shoes. A gimmick to consider for a short day's outing is to encase the socked foot in a plastic bag (the bag goes between the outer sock and the shoe). Though your socks will be wet with perspiration at the day's end, your feet will have remained warm throughout the course of a short day's tramp.

Pants: Non-constricting pants of dense wool, or synthetic pile or fleece make for an excellent insulating layer. Some snowshoers opt for expedition-weight synthetic longjohns for the second level. Wool or fleece knickers are also popular for winter sports. Deep, strong pockets that close are more than a convenience for winter sportspeople and a sturdy belt is an advisable accessory.

Shirt/Sweater: Wool or a heavy synthetic shirt, and a light fleece sweater (100-200 weight) are ideal for one-day trippers. A thick pile or fleece hooded jacket (300 weight) or, even better, a down jacket with attached hood, is recommended for snow campers. All insulating garments should be simple to don or remove, and the successive layers should not restrict easy movement.

Neck Gaiter: Polypropylene or fleece neck warmers double and triple as hats, earmuffs, or even balaclavas. Thin silk or polypropylene neck gaiters can provide an extra layer of warmth under a hat or hood in severe weather. Silk balaclavas also serve in that capacity.

Hat: A warm, brimmed, ear-protective hat of wool, felt, synthetic fleece, or insulated fabric is an absolute must in the winter wild. Since up to seventy percent of body heat may be dissipated by a bare head, lost skiers have died for want of a hat. For full sun protection, a brim is essential in snow country unless you are wearing totally enclosed goggles. A second lightweight tennis hat or a visor is strongly advised for those periods of activity when the going is hot. A balaclava is comforting during cold snaps and in snow camps. A second warm hat is advisable for snow campers.

Gloves: Over-the-glove liners, an array of insulating gloves are available—wool (particularly boiled wool), insulated water-resistant leather (leather gloves are difficult to waterproof fully), and fleece in a variety of synthetics. The choice is personal, but do not buy gloves that do not dry easily and/or do not keep your hands warm when wet. Fingerless gloves are useful when repairing equipment or for close work around camp. One way to beat the high cost of camping is to buy inexpensive garden or work gloves and cut off the fingertips to whatever length suits you best. Wool or fleece gloves should have rubber, leather or leather-like strips or dots on the palms for a good grip. Mittens are warmer than gloves.

Outer Layer

Gaiters: Waterproof gaiters should cover the leg from the lowest shoe lace on your boot to the knee. Gaiters should be easy on-easy off, and should have some tightening device at the top to ensure "stay-up" over the course of a strenuous day. Mini-gaiters (low gaiters) may look cute but they do little good in heavy snow. For really frigid weather, insulated gaiters are available.

Pants: Windproof/waterproof pants which pass perspiration through but keep rain out (waterproof/breathable) are markedly superior to waterproof non-breathable fabrics. Snowshoers and skiers work up a full sweat on the trail and need garments which will transport perspiration out from the body. Coated nylon materials will keep the rain out, but after a full day in the snow such garments will be dripping with sweat.

Choose pants which go on or off easily over boots. Many pants with short zippers or snap arrangements will go on (or off) over shoes, but only after a tussle. For the sake of tranquillity and composure, avoid such garments. Good pants should have extra protection at abrasion-prone areas. If one can swallow the price tag, a rainproof breathable pair of pants with a full zipper (top to bottom) is a great convenience on the trail, and covered, closeable pockets are another useful feature.

Jackets: Breathable rainproof jackets are an even greater requisite than their accompanying pants. The torso is particularly vulnerable to cold and consequent hypothermia, and must be protected. The jacket should be large enough to accommodate the insulating clothing, and long enough to cover well below the belt line. The jacket should be long enough to resist riding up under a backpack. A full-length zipper for easy on/off, and fully protected outside pockets as well as sturdy inside storage pockets are the mark of a well-designed jacket. An attached hood is a must, preferably one that provides full vision with full protection.

Non-breathable waterproof jackets, such as polyurethane coated nylon, will do an excellent job of keeping the rain out, but wearers should anticipate a heavy sweat build-up inside the jacket — enough to saturate the insulating layer below.

Hats: The waterproof hood on the jacket serves best as the outside layer for the head. However, many hats are designed to act as both the insulating layer and the windproof shell. If you carry only one such hat, however, you lose versatility in dress. The best advice is to carry a lightweight balaclava as the base layer in cold weather, a warm hat with a brim sufficient to shield the eyes, a lightweight, brimmed tennis hat for eye protection during the sweaty stretches and, as mentioned, the hood of your jacket as it may be needed.

Gloves: Nylon quick-drying shells, either gloves or mittens, or waterproof breathable mittens provide the requisite outer cover for the hands. Many shell-type fabrics may be made near-waterproof with brush on solutions such as Aqua-seal or Nikwax. Gloves take a beating in normal wear and should be made of abrasion-resistant fabrics with palms designed to grip metal and other such smooth equipment.

All winter garments should accommodate the next underlayer easily, with no extra bulk or bagginess. Constricting clothes impede both insulation and movement and should be rejected—shun any and all Spandex!

3 ❄
Gear for Snowshoers, Nordic Skiers, Snow Campers

In addition to the equipment normally carried by hikers or backpackers, winter sports groups should carry gear designed specifically for snow and cold weather emergencies. Most of these items should be carried by each member of the party, but, at discretion, some items may be distributed at less than one for every trekker.

Map(s) and Compass: Snow hikers, snowshoers, or Nordic skiers must be particularly adept in their ability to lay out a route devoid of trail markers and to find the way home.

Special Tape: To supplement the map and compass, highly visible, fluorescent-like pink or yellow survey tape can be tied to tree branches along a route to expedite the way back. It can serve also as a signal communications device among groups split off from the main party—"We went that-a-way." If you use survey tape, be sure to remove every strip on the return trip.

Snow Shovel: In an actual test, a group of skiers was assembled to excavate a one cubic meter (35 cubic feet) hole in a mound of fresh avalanche debris. They first dug using only hands, skis, and poles; the average time was 45 minutes. The second time they dug with a shovel; the average time, 8 minutes—five times faster! Moral:

Make sure you have a snow shovel on your winter hikes. Excellent lightweight aluminum, Lexan, or other polycarbonate shovels are available. Almost all the shovels collapse for ease in carrying. A typical plastic shovel weighs less than 24 ounces.

Snow Probe: Collapsible probe poles, ten to twelve feet long when extended, are recommended for backcountry snow trekkers, particularly for groups headed for avalanche territory. Some snowshoe or ski poles are designed with removable grips and baskets. When snapped or screwed together, depending on the model, a set of these poles acts as a probe.

First Aid Kit: A good backpacking first aid kit, supplemented by elastic tape for sprained ankles; heat packs for hands, feet, and body; glucose for prevention or treatment of hypothermia; electrolytes for rehydration; and waterproof/windproof matches is advised for the backcountry snow hiker. Several companies make good first aid kits, and Atwater Carey (Boulder, Colorado) which makes customized kits for particular sports, will provide their "Walkabout Kit," supplemented as noted, customized for snowshoers, Nordic skiers, and snow campers.

Multiple Purpose Tool: A single lightweight tool with pliers, screw drivers, file, knives, and other implements is basic insurance for snow trips. The Leatherman Survival Tool is one of the most imitated instruments on the market, but its quality is unsurpassed, except, perhaps, by the Leatherman Super Tool which provides two additional tools and several more functions. The smallest member of this elegant family is the Mini-Tool (with pliers also), far better than a pocket knife for each member of the group.

Duct Tape: The everything remedy from foot blisters to broken ski poles. It deserves its reputation as the required *vade mecum* of the outdoors. Never enter the woods without it. Strapping tape is also useful for a variety of quick repair situations.

Metal Cup: A one-pint cup with folding handles that can sit right over a flame is the right choice for winter snow outings. Some of these cups come with lids, which help speed the snow-to-boiled-water process. Note: Never eat snow or ice when fatigued. Melting snow in the mouth requires more energy than your body can afford, and it cools the body internally. Drink lots of water. High energy exercise creates a perspiration loss of two to four quarts in a day, and failure to replace that loss will result in extreme fatigue.

Candles: Long-burning candles are recommended. Some trekkers prefer canned heat such as "Cook n' Heat" or a multiple wick candle such as Newick. The wicks sit in a lidded metal can of paraffin, and may be moved and lit singly for illumination, or doubly or triply for heat and cooking.

Emergency Blanket: For one-day trips, the two-ounce Space Emergency Blanket (56″ x 84″ aluminized sheet), originally developed as a super insulator for NASA, is a recommended choice. For longer trips, the more versatile (groundsheet, tarp, sunshade, waterproof cover, blanket) ten-ounce, All Weather Blanket (56″ x 81″ four-layer, aluminum sheet and fabric backing between plastic film leaves) should be considered. Both blankets act to reflect up to 80% of radiated body heat back to the body. When you are cold and fatigued, the blanket should be worn, metallic side in, over the head, with legs drawn up to the chest in a fetal position, to conserve as much body heat as possible. In case of an accident, after caring for any possible wound, wrap the patient in the blanket to help prevent post trauma shock. Both blankets reflect radar, and may be used for emergency signaling.

Signal Mirror: It is claimed that a signal mirror flash can be seen as much as 100 miles away. Whatever the validity of that claim, a good mirror, such as the Gerber (Portland, Oregon) is worth its weight (seven-tenths of an ounce) in self assurance alone. The Safe Signal (Tucson, Arizona) one-and-a-half ounces in its neoprene, floating, velcro carrying case may be used conventionally, or in conjunction with a flashlight for night signaling.

Heat Packs: Heat packs are now available for body, hands, and feet. Each pack will keep you warm for a couple of hours.

Plastic Garbage Bags: Along with duct tape, the large plastic garbage bag has become the most popular take along item for snow outings. Waterproof emergency clothes, ground sheet, pack cover, tarp, waterproof stuff-bag—you name it, the plastic bag can do it.

Whistle: A whistle screech carries further than human voices.

4 ❄
Winter Hazards

Avalanches

There are several types of avalanches—snow, ice, rock, and mud. Throughout this section, we shall discuss snow avalanches exclusively, and the information presented is derived from a variety of U.S. Forest Service publications. Snow avalanches, even small avalanches, can hold mammoth power and represent a serious threat to winter sports enthusiasts. Naturally, the more time one spends in snow backcountry, the greater are the chances of being caught in an avalanche. To avoid possible capture by a snow slide, one should know the types of avalanches, terrain, and weather conditions which contribute to such disasters, and the safest terrain in crossing avalanche territory. Such knowledge will assist the winter recreationist to steer clear of snow slides, and even to survive if buried by such a snow torrent.

The two basic types of avalanches are "loose snow" and "slab." Loose snow avalanches start at a small area or a single point. The snow volume increases as does the area covered as the loose snow descends, forming an inverted V. There is little internal cohesion in a loose snow slide, and the snow plunges as a formless mass.

Slab avalanches, on the other hand, start when a large area of snow begins to slide at once. There is a well-defined fracture line where the moving snow breaks away from the stable snow. Slab avalanches are characterized by the tendency of snow crystals to stick together. There may be angular blocks or chunks of snow in the slide. Practically all accidents are caused by slab avalanches. Many times the victims have triggered the avalanche themselves. Their weight on the stressed snow slab is enough to break the fragile bonds that hold it to the slope.

TERRAIN FACTORS

There are four terrain factors affecting snow avalanches: slope steepness, slope profile, slope aspect, and ground cover.

Slope steepness. Avalanches are most common on slopes of 30 to 45 degrees (60 to 100 percent), but large avalanches can occur on slopes ranging from 25 to 60 degrees. The diagram below shows the slopes where avalanches are most common.

Slope profile. Dangerous slab avalanches are more likely to occur on convex slopes, but may also occur on concave slopes. Short slopes may be as dangerous as long slopes!

Slope aspect. Snow on north-facing slopes is more likely to slide in midwinter. South-facing slopes are dangerous in the spring and on sunny days. Leeward slopes are dangerous because wind-deposited snows add depth and create hard, hollow-sounding wind slabs. Windward slopes, generally, have less snow, the snow is compacted, and usually strong enough to resist movement.

Ground cover. Large rocks, trees, and heavy brush help anchor the snow, but avalanches can start even among trees. Smooth, grassy slopes are more dangerous.

Rule of Thumb: If, on skis, you can move through a wooded area, so can an avalanche.

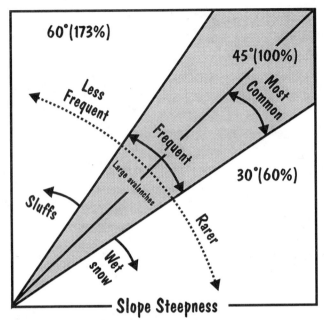

60°(173%)

45°(100%)

Less Frequent

Most Common

Frequent

Large avalanches

30°(60%)

Sluffs

Rarer

Wet snow

Slope Steepness

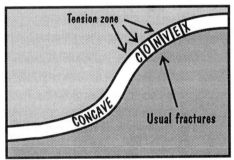

Tension zone

CONVEX

CONCAVE

Usual fractures

Snow is anchored

Snow slides easily

WEATHER FACTORS

Many weather factors affect the chances of a snow avalanche occurring: temperature, wind, storms, rate of snowfall, and types of snow.

Temperature. Snow persists in an unstable condition under cold temperatures. It will settle and stabilize rapidly when temperatures are near, or just above, freezing. Storms starting with low temperatures and dry snow, followed by rising temperatures, are more likely to cause avalanches. The dry snow at the start forms a poor bond and has insufficient strength to support the heavier snow deposited late in the storm. Rapid changes in weather conditions (wind, temperature, snowfall) cause snowpack adjustments. Such adjustments may affect snowpack stability and cause an avalanche. Therefore, be alert to weather changes.

Wind. Sustained winds of 15 miles per hour and over rapidly increase the danger of an avalanche occurring. Snow plumes from ridges and peaks indicate that snow is being moved onto leeward

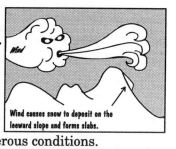

Wind causes snow to deposit on the leeward slope and forms slabs.

slopes. This can create dangerous conditions.

Storms. A high percentage (about 80 percent) of all avalanches occur during, and shortly after, storms. Be extra cautious during those periods. Loose, dry snow slides easily. Moist, dense snow tends to settle rapidly, but during windy periods can be dangerous.

Rate of snowfall. Snow falling at the rate of one inch per hour or more rapidly increases avalanche danger.

Crystal types. Snow crystal types may be examined by letting them fall on a dark ski mitt or parka sleeve. Small crystals—needles and pellets—result in more dangerous conditions than star-shaped crystals.

For weather information, check the local weather forecasts. Contact the Forest Service snow ranger or the nearest winter sports area ski patrol.

GENERAL OBSERVATIONS

Look for signs of recent avalanche activity and old slide paths; listen for sounds and cracks; be alert to snow conditions.

Recent avalanche activity. If you see new avalanche evidence, suspect dangerous conditions. Beware when snowballs or "cartwheels" roll down the slope.

Old slide paths. Generally, avalanches occur in the same areas. Watch for avalanche paths. Look for pushed-over small trees, trees with limbs broken off. Avoid steep, open gullies, and slopes.

Sounds and cracks. If the snow sounds hollow, particularly on a leeward slope, conditions are probably dangerous. If the snow cracks and the cracks continue to form, this indicates slab avalanche danger is high.

New snow. Be alert to dangerous conditions with one foot or more of new snow.

Old snow. When the old snow depth is sufficient to cover natural anchors—such as rocks and brush—additional snow layers will slide more readily. The nature of the old snow surface is important. Rough surfaces favor stability; smooth surfaces, such as sun crusts, are less stable. A loose, underlying snow layer is more dangerous than a compacted one. Check the underlying snow layer with a ski pole, ski, or rod.

Wet snow. Rainstorms or spring weather with warm winds and cloudy nights can warm snow cover. The resulting free and percolating water may cause wet snow avalanches. Wet snow avalanches are more likely on south slopes and slopes under exposed rock.

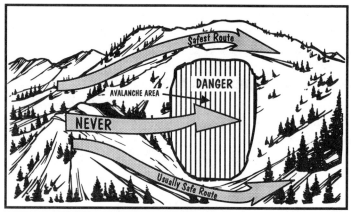

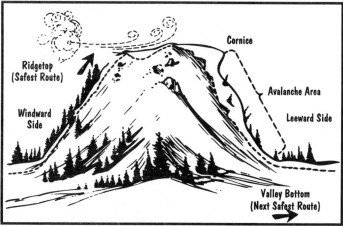

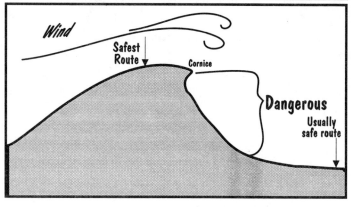

ROUTE SELECTION AND PRECAUTIONS

The safest routes are on ridgetops and slightly on the windward side, away from cornices. Windward slopes are usually safer than leeward slopes. If you cannot travel on the ridges, the next safest route is out in the valley, far from the bottom of slopes. Avoid disturbing cornices from below or above. Gain ridgetops by detouring around cornice areas. If you must cross dangerous slopes, stay high and near the top. If you see avalanche fracture lines in the snow, avoid them and similar snow areas. If you must ascend or descend a dangerous slope, go straight up or down; do not make traverses back and forth across the slope. Take advantage of areas of dense timber, ridges, or rocky outcrops as islands of safety. Use them for lunch and rest stops. Spend as little time as possible on open slopes.

Obey signs closing slopes due to avalanche danger. Only one person at a time should cross a dangerous slope. All others should watch him. Remove ski pole straps, ski safety straps, loosen all equipment, put on mittens and cap, and fasten clothing before you travel in any areas where there is avalanche danger. Carry and use an avalanche cord; carry a sectional probe.

AVALANCHE SURVIVAL

If you are caught in an avalanche:
• Discard all equipment.
• Make swimming motions. Try to stay on top; work your way to the side of the avalanche.
• Before coming to a stop, get your hands in front of your face and try to make an air space in the snow as you are coming to a stop.
• Try to remain calm.
If you are the survivor:
• Mark the place where you last saw victims.

- Search for victims directly downslope below the last seen point. If they are not on the surface, probe the snow with a pole or stick.
- You are the victim's best hope for survival.
- Do not desert victims and go for help, unless help is only a few minutes away. Remember you must consider not only the time required to get help, but the time required to return. After 30 minutes, the buried victim has only a 50 percent chance of surviving.

If there is more than one survivor:
- Send one for help while the others search for the victim. Have the one who goes for help mark the route so a rescue party can follow back.
- Contact the ski patrol, local sheriff, or Forest Service.
- Administer first aid.
- Treat for suffocation and shock.

Travel on Ice

Travel over frozen lakes, ponds or streams may be hazardous. If you are the least bit uncertain, assume that the ice is unsafe. The Cold Region Research and Engineering Laboratory in Hanover, New Hampshire, recommends the following basic rules. The pond or lake ice should be at least two inches thick to support one person on a ten-foot-square section, and four inches thick for two persons. When out with a group, watch for cracks. If possible, drill a hole in the ice and take note of the water level. If the water reaches the top of the ice and begins to spill over, all group members should slowly walk toward land. Do not run because running can create waves which fracture the ice. Most important: use common sense and do not go out alone.

Hypothermia

Be aware of the danger of hypothermia—subnormal temperature of the body. Lowering of internal temperature of the body leads to mental and physical collapse. Hypothermia is caused by exposure to cold, and is aggravated by wet, wind, and exhaustion. It is the number one killer of outdoor recreationists.

SEVEN STEPS TO HYPOTHERMIA
How The Body Loses Heat

1. **Radiation.** Heat loss through the skin. The head is the greatest radiator. Wear a hat!

2. **Conduction.** Touching cold surfaces such as snow, ice, metals, and fuels. Wear gloves!

3. **Convection.** Wind moves warm air quickly from clothing and body. Wear windproof clothes and get out of the wind!

4. **Evaporation.** Fast, excessive sweat loss. Wear clothes that get perspiration off the skin. Avoid undue sweating by adjusting layers of clothes. Keep warm, but try not to sweat excessively.

5. **Respiration.** Inhaling cold air and exhaling warm air causes great internal heat loss. In severe weather, breathe in through a headband and out through the mouth.

6. **Wind Chill.** Accompanying wind magnifies the severity of cold temperatures. A breeze of only 2 miles per hour can greatly increase perceived cold. Wear windproof clothes and get out of the wind.

7. **Water Chill.** The thermal conductivity of water is 240 times that of still air! Wet clothing can extract heat 240 times faster than dry clothes! Water is considered one of nature's greatest conductors of heat. Change out of wet clothes as soon as possible.

COLD KILLS IN TWO DISTINCT STEPS

The first step is exposure and exhaustion. The moment you begin to lose heat faster than your body produces it, you are undergoing exposure. Two things happen: you voluntarily exercise to stay warm, and your body makes involuntary adjustments to preserve normal temperature in the vital organs. Both responses drain your energy reserves. The only way to stop the drain is to reduce the degree of exposure. The time to prevent hypothermia is during this period of exposure and gradual exhaustion.

The second step is hypothermia. If exposure continues until your energy reserves are exhausted, cold reaches the brain, depriving you of judgment and reasoning power. You will not be aware that this is happening. You will lose control of your hands. This is hypothermia. Your internal temperature is sliding downward. Without treatment, this slide leads to stupor, collapse, and death.

WIND CHILL

Wind, temperature, and moisture are factors which can greatly affect the safety of a winter traveler. Each contributes to the loss of body heat. The "wind chill" chart illustrates the effect of wind and temperatures on a dry, properly clothed person. If clothing is wet from perspiration or precipitation, the net effect of wind and temperature is much greater.

SYMPTOMS

If your party is exposed to wind, cold and wet, **think hypothermia**. Watch yourself and others for symptoms.
• Uncontrollable fits of shivering.
• Vague, slow, slurred speech.
• Memory lapses, incoherence.
• Immobile, fumbling hands.

Wind Speed Cooling Power Expressed as "Equivalent Temperature"

mph	Temperature (F)											
Calm	40	30	20	10	5	0	-10	-20	-30	-40	-50	-60
	Equivalent Chill Temperature											
5	35	25	15	5	0	-5	-15	-25	-35	-45	-55	-70
10	30	15	5	-10	-15	-20	-35	-45	-60	-70	-80	-95
15	25	10	-5	-20	-25	-30	-45	-60	-70	-85	-100	-110
20	20	5	-10	-25	-30	-35	-50	-65	-80	-95	-110	-120
25	15	0	-15	-30	-35	-45	-60	-75	-90	-105	-120	-135
30	10	0	-20	-30	-40	-50	-65	-80	-95	-110	-125	-140
35	10	-5	-20	-35	-40	-50	-65	-80	-100	-115	-130	-145
40	10	-5	-20	-35	-45	-55	-70	-85	-100	-115	-130	-150
	Danger			Increasing Danger (Flesh may freeze within 1 minute)				Great Danger (Flesh may freeze within 30 seconds)				

Example: At a wind speed of 20 mph, an ambient temperature of 20 degrees Fahrenheit is equivalent to minus 10 degrees Fahrenheit.

- Frequent stumbling. Lurching gait.
- Drowsiness — to sleep is to die.
- Apparent exhaustion. Inability to get up after a rest.

TREATMENT

The victim may deny he is in trouble. Believe the symptoms, not the victim. Even mild symptoms demand immediate, drastic treatment.

- Get the victim out of the wind and rain.
- Strip off all wet clothes.
- If the victim is only mildly impaired, give him warm drinks. Get him into warm clothes and a warm sleeping bag. Well-wrapped, warm (not hot) rocks or canteens will hasten recovery.

- If the victim is semi-conscious or worse, try to keep him awake. Give him warm drinks. Leave him stripped. Put the victim in a sleeping bag with another person—also stripped. If you have a double bag, put the victim between two warm donors. Skin to skin contact is the most effective treatment.
- Build a fire to warm the camp.

PREVENTION—DEFENSE AGAINST HYPOTHERMIA

Stay dry. When clothes get wet, they lose about 90 percent of their insulating value. Wool and some synthetics lose less; cotton and down lose more. Choose rainclothes that are proof against wind-driven rain and cover head, neck, body, and legs. Breathable waterproof garments are best. Polyurethane coated nylon will keep the rain out, but it will keep the perspiration in, and the coatings won't last forever. Inspect coated nylon garments carefully and test under a cold shower before you leave home. Ponchos are poor protection from the wind.

Beware of the wind. A slight breeze carries heat away from bare skin much faster than still air. Wind drives cold air under and through clothing. Wind refrigerates wet clothes by evaporating moisture from the surface. Wind multiplies the problem of staying dry. Take synthetic fleece or woolen clothing for hypothermia weather. Wear two-piece synthetic underwear, long wool pants and a sweater or shirt. Include a hat or balaclava that can protect neck and chin. Cotton underwear is worse than useless when wet; cotton kills!

Understand cold. Most hypothermia cases develop in air temperatures between 30 and 50 degrees. Most outdoorsmen can't believe such temperatures can be dangerous. They underestimate the danger of being wet at such temperatures—with fatal results. Fifty-degree water is unbearably cold. The cold that kills is cold water running down neck and legs and cold water held against the body by wet clothes, flushing heat from the body.

Use your clothes. Put on raingear before you get wet. Put on warm clothes before you start shivering.

End exposure. If you cannot stay dry and warm under existing weather conditions, using the clothes you have with you, end your exposure to the elements immediately. Be smart enough to forego reaching the peak or making that last run or whatever else may entice you to stay out when wet or cold.

Get out of the wind and rain. Build a fire. Concentrate on making your camp or bivouac as secure and comfortable as possible. Never ignore shivering. Persistent or violent shivering is clear warning that you are on the verge of hypothermia. A stormproof tent gives best shelter. Take plastic sheeting and nylon twine with you for rigging additional foul-weather shelter.

Carry trail food—nuts, jerky, candy—and keep nibbling during hypothermia weather. Take a camp stove or a long burning candle, flammable paste, or other reliable firestarters. Don't wait for an emergency. Use these items to avoid or minimize exposure. Take heed of "hypothermia weather." Watch carefully for warning symptoms. Choose equipment with hypothermia in mind. Think hypothermia.

Forestall exhaustion. Make camp while you still have a reserve of energy and allow for the fact that exposure greatly reduces your normal endurance. Be aware that exercise drains energy reserves. If exhaustion forces you to stop, however briefly, your body heat production instantly drops 50 percent or more. Violent, incapacitating shivering may begin immediately, and you may slip into hypothermia in a matter of minutes.

Appoint a foul-weather leader. Make the best-protected member of your party responsible for calling a halt before the least-protected member becomes exhausted or goes into violent shivering.

Dehydration

An adult at rest requires 2 quarts of water daily. Up to 4 quarts are required for strenuous activity. There is a 25% loss of stamina when an adult loses 1½ quarts of water. Avoid dehydration—drink as often as you feel thirsty. Better yet, drink before you get thirsty.

Frostbite

Frostbite is caused by exposure of inadequately protected flesh to subfreezing temperatures. Tissue damage is caused by the reduced blood flow to the extremities as opposed to hypothermia, which causes lowering of the body's rate of metabolism.

SYMPTOMS

Mild: Redness, inflammation, stinging.
Moderate: Skin gray or mottled white and soft to pressure, intense stinging.
Severe: Skin waxy white, hard or stiff, swollen, loss of sensation.

TREATMENT

Restore body temperature as rapidly as possible, preferably by immersion in a water bath of less than 11 0 temperature, by hot coffee or tea, or by other means. If necessary to continue the trek, the affected part should be kept dry and covered and the victim moved as quickly as possible to a location where effective treatment and/or vehicle evacuation can be obtained.

Most frequently, isolated parts of the body: cheeks, nose, hands and feet are subject to frostbite. Gently cover ears and nose with warm hands. If feet are frostbitten, place cotton between the toes and try to keep the victim from placing weight on the foot. Never attempt to rewarm the affected area by rubbing or massaging, and do not allow the sufferer to smoke (nicotine constricts arteries and hinders blood flow). Bear in mind that the patient may experience severe pain as the affected part thaws and recovers.

PREVENTION

Party members should periodically observe their companions, especially nose and cheeks, for signs of frostbite. Snowmobilers, due to their speed of travel, are particularly susceptible to frostbite.

Altitude Sickness

At 10,000 feet, air contains only two-thirds of the volume of oxygen that it does at sea level. In addition, the higher air pressure at sea level easily forces the available oxygen through the thin lining of the lungs into the bloodstream. At higher elevations there is less air pressure and it is more difficult for the available oxygen to be forced through the lung walls.

SYMPTOMS

Nausea, dizziness, fatigue and drowsiness as well as weakness, apathy, listlessness and loss of appetite.

TREATMENT

Stop and rest, breathe deeply several times, obtain nourishment from simple sugar, like candy or fruit juices. Take aspirin or ibuprofen and travel as soon as possible to lower elevations. If possible, spend a night at an intermediate elevation between home and destination. Acclimate yourself with a day of light exercise at the higher elevation before a major trip, and try to limit your ascent to less than 2000 feet a day on your trip. Altitude sickness or acute mountain sickness is not life threatening and sufferers will recover after a few uncomfortable days, provided they move to lower altitudes. (Note: Two other altitude-associated illnesses, pulmonary edema and cerebral edema, are almost always associated with extreme heights, over 14,000 feet, and can be life threatening.)

PREVENTION

Keep in good physical condition and eat a well-balanced diet. Avoid sudden trips which involve immediate physical exercise to high altitudes.

Hyperventilation

SYMPTOMS

This reaction to altitude is caused by too rapid breathing and decrease of the carbon dioxide level in the blood, causing light-headedness and a sense of cold. Victims are apprehensive and excited.

TREATMENT

Calm the victim, have him relax and breathe into a glove, bag, or hat until normal breathing is restored.

PREVENTION

Same as for altitude sickness.

Lost or Injured Party

A good map, skill with a compass, and pre-planning will minimize the possibility of getting lost. Check weather forecasts and avoid storms. It is easy to become disoriented in the whiteouts of winter or when physically exhausted.

Keep calm. Decide on a plan. Trust your compass. Backtrack if possible. If impractical, remain in place.

Stay together if possible. If not, send at least two people for help.
• Don't abandon your snowshoes or skis.
• Build a fire and shelter.
• Stay warm.
• Mark your base camp so it is visible from the air.

DISTRESS SIGNALS

Three smokes, three blasts of a whistle, three shouts, three flashes of light, three of anything that will attract attention.

GROUND TO AIR SIGNALS

Visible emergency signals are easily made in large open areas. SOS can be stamped in snowfields or grassy meadows. Brush piles or evergreen boughs can also be used. Listed below is the emergency code for ground to air signals.

I	II	X
Require doctor— serious injury	Require medical supplies	Unable to proceed
F	V	↑
Require food and water	Require assistance	Proceeding in this direction
Y	N	LL
Yes—affirmative	No—negative	All well

OVERDUE PARTY

When Someone Is Overdue.—*Keep calm.* Notify the County Sheriff or District Ranger in the trip area. Either of these officers will take steps to alert or activate the local search and rescue organization. If the missing person returns later, be sure to advise the Sheriff or Ranger.

BACKCOUNTRY SAFETY

• Never travel alone.

• Select a travel route familiar to at least one member of your party and equal to your experience and ability.

• Consult a ranger station for the weather forecast, snow and avalanche conditions, touring routes, and equipment recommendations before departing.

• Postpone or terminate your trip if a storm is forecast or appears to be building.

• If caught in a storm, wait it out in a sheltered, avalanche-safe area until conditions stabilize.

• Be prepared for winter weather extremes (gale winds, sub-zero temperatures, blowing snow, white-out conditions) which can kill the unprepared.

• Allow extra travel time during soft snow conditions.

• Keep a written note of the nearest ranger station or emergency telephone number for use in emergencies.

• **Remember you are dependent on your own good sense and resources for survival.**

5 ❄
Snowmobile Safety

Snowmobiling is hazardous, and a safety course for beginners is a wise precaution. Snowmobilers require specialized clothing for added protection.

Clothing

The layering system described in Chapter 2 is also recommended for snowmobilers except that the final "shell" layer may be a heavier, special snowmobile suit. Such suits may be lined with flotation material in case your vehicle breaks through the ice over a waterway. Some suits have a flotation device which can be inflated with a few quick puffs. Headgear must include an approved helmet, but avoid the bubble type of face guards as they may frost over. Goggles are a must since they act as sun shields and protect the eyes against snow, cold, tree branches, and other such obstructions. They also protect against snow blindness, and protective lenses can prevent freezing of the eyeballs. Green or grey/brown lenses are recommended for day driving, but clear lenses should be used at night.

A scarf is not recommended for snowmobilers because the ends may get caught in the machinery. Use a versatile neck-gaiter which will serve a variety of uses. For handwarmers, mittens are the warmest. Gloves or mittens should not fit tightly, nor have a shell that gets stiff when cold. Insulated ski gloves are preferred by some and are fine if you find them comfortable. However, you should always carry an extra pair of mittens. A light inner glove or liner prevents freezing of the skin if you must remove outer mittens to handle small items.

Your feet need high-bulk wool or fleece socks worn in a good boot. It is always a good idea to have an extra pair on any trip far from home. Be sure your socks do not create too tight a fit for that will cut off circulation—a common cause of cold feet. Boots must keep your feet warm and dry even though you do little walking. Rubber-bottomed boots with felt liners are popular with snow-mobilers. Moon boots are also popular.

Safety Equipment

Safety and emergency equipment vary with the terrain and the mileage of your intended trip. Always keep your operator's manual and pre-gapped spark plugs in a handy compartment. Bear in mind that it can take a full day's walk to cover the distance traveled in one hour on the snowmobile. Every snowmobiler should carry these basic parts and tools in the event of a mechanical failure:
• Screwdrivers (including a Phillips)
• Locking pliers
• Adjustable wrench
• Black electrical tape
• Set of open end wrenches

Also prepare for an emergency. Provide for a return on foot from a disabled machine.
• Map and compass
• First aid kit
• 100 feet of nylon rope (¼ inch or more)
• Waterproof matches
• High energy foods (at least a one day supply)
• A pair of snowshoes
• Flashlight and extra batteries

- Flares
- Emergency shelter (tube tent, tarp)
- Space blanket and/or emergency blanket
- Sunblock cream (SPF 30 or above)
- Duct tape
- Expanded tool kit (including special wrenches and a spark plug socket)
- Fuel hose (long enough to be used as a siphon)
- Knife/ax
- Wristwatch

For added safety, you should also consider some extra items such as a camp stove, fuel, a one-quart pot and a radio (for storm warnings). If a fire is required, you can use fuel and/or oil drained from your snowmobile to aid in igniting wet wood. If your matches are wet, it is possible to start a fire using your snowmobile's ignition system. Remove a spark plug, re-attach the plug wire to the plug, ground the plug against the snowmobile, crank the engine, and a spark will be created. Use extreme caution. Do not create an unmanageable fire.

Emergency Action

If your snowmobile breaks down and you are unable to walk out, you must conserve energy in order to survive. As a rule of thumb, consider that it may take a full day to hike the distance that you can travel in one hour on your snowmobile. Your machine can be used as a windbreak or as part of a lean-to. Seek shelter from the wind in a protected area. An overhanging rock shelf, or a clearing at the base of a tree make good starting points for shelter.

In a timbered area, you can make a lean-to by placing horizontal bars between two trees or upright poles, and lean small branches against the horizontal bar. Interweave the branches to strengthen the shelter. Snow

banks and deep drifts offer protection possibilities. Dig a
snow cave (or **Quinzee**) facing away from the wind,
slightly larger than your body size. Line the cave with any
extra material you may have, such as snowmobile seats.
Be sure to pierce a six-inch diameter ventilating hole in
the top of the cave.

Systematic maintenance of the machine, travel with
a companion and, in particular, good pre-planning will
minimize the possibility of emergencies.

1. Prepare a checklist and check it prior to departure.
2. Leave word with a responsible party of planned departure and return times. If possible, leave similar information at the appropriate ranger station.
3. If a fire is needed (and possible), choose a protected
   spot away from overhanging snow-laden branches. If
   sufficient appropriate down-wood is available, collect
   enough fuel before dark to keep the fire going all night
4. Do not travel on foot in strange areas. Conserve your
   energy. Moderate exercise to keep warm is acceptable,
   but don't overexert. Common sense is the best companion in an emergency. If you become unsure of your location during a heavy snowstorm or blizzard, stop, find
   shelter, and keep warm.
5. In every situation, attend to injuries first, then stop,
   observe, and plan solutions and possibilities. Panic is
   the enemy.

When and if you decide to remain in one place and
allow rescuers to find you, certain steps must be taken.

Display the signals shown above. Use colored cloth
or paper cutouts, or stamp out a signal in the snow. Make
the signs as large as possible, about 18 feet high and three
feet wide, so they can be spotted from the air easily. On a
sunny day, a signal mirror or anything with a reflecting
surface is the best signal you can use. Signal with it as
often as possible.

Cold Water Exposure

Snowmobiling on and around frozen water is possible with proper knowledge and precautions; without them, a frigid dunking can prove fatal. Specialists in physiology have determined the following "safe" immersion times for the unprotected human body:

Water Temperature

At 40 degrees or lower .... Less than 10 minutes
40-50 degrees .... 5 to 20 minutes
50-60 degrees .... 40 minutes
Above 60 degrees .... 1 hour or more

Beyond these limits even a well-conditioned athlete will soon lose all ability to cling to anything for support, and rescue must depend completely upon others.

If such a rescue should be necessary, the victim's wet clothing should be removed immediately and the person should be "sandwiched" between two dry companions who have also disrobed. Any available blankets or clothing should then be wrapped around all three people. This massive application of warmth to a great part of a victim's body is the only protection against the phenomenon known as "after cooling" when the constricted outer blood vessels relax in the first relief from frigid water and permit supercooled blood to flow back to the heart, sometimes causing it to fail. Other rescuers should meanwhile prepare hot beverages and a fire for warmth, but because of timing, this step is secondary.

Proper dress can eliminate the need for emergency measures. Wool and some synthetic clothes are preferred to other fabrics since they provide some insulation even when wet. A complete change of dry clothing in a waterproof pack is a good safety precaution. However, the best protection is provided by a wetsuit. The style and thickness should be determined by the degree of protection desired. Since there is considerable heat loss from the top of the head, a wool cap or fleece balaclava should be worn under the helmet. Helmets offer additional protection.

Winter Hazards

For avalanche, hypothermia, frostbite and other winter emergencies, see the earlier chapter on winter hazards. Snowmobile safe routes are the same as those for snowshoers and skiers, but snowmobilers must be particularly careful in avalanche country because of the weight and sound level of the machines. Do not drive across the lower parts of slopes and never drive across long open slopes or known avalanche paths. If you are caught in an avalanche, get away from your machine as soon as possible and follow the avalanche instructions given earlier.

Snowmobile Safety Code

1. Bring your snowmobile to top mechanical condition at the beginning of the winter season and throughout the months of use.
2. Familiarize yourself with thoroughly with the operator's manual.
3. Wear protective clothing designed specifically for snowmobiling.
4. Use a full helmet, goggles or face shield to prevent injuries from twigs, stones, ice chips and flying debris.
5. Shun long scarves. They may get caught in the snowmobile's moving parts. (Remember Ruth St. Denis.)
6. Know the terrain you plan to ride, particularly the ice and snow conditions. If unfamiliar, consult an area veteran.
7. Heed the weather forecast. Keep a weather eye out, and be prepared to beat a retreat at the first sign of dirty weather.

8. Always use the buddy system. Never ride solo.
9. Drowning is a rising cause of snowmobile fatalities. Avoid waterways unless you are 100% familiar with the ice and water currents.
10. Leave the factory-installed muffler intact. A higher decibel muffler lowers the performance of your vehicle and adds disagreeable racket to the wilderness.

SNOWMOBILE TRAIL SIGNS

When riding your snowmobile, you will encounter trail signs. They are designed to communicate information about the trail to you. Below are some of the most common trail signs for you to learn.

REGULATORY

STOP SIGN
PURPOSE: To be used along trails prior to a road crossing.
SIZE: 12"x12"
BACKGROUND COLOR: Red
BORDER AND LEGEND: Silver

STOP AHEAD SIGN
PURPOSE: To indicate the snowmobiler must stop ahead.
BACKGROUND COLOR AND LEGEND: Yellow with black lettering

TRAILHEAD MARKER
PURPOSE: To indicate snowmobile trailheads and other areas permitting snowmobiling.
BACKGROUND COLOR AND LEGEND: Brown with white border and white snowmobile symbol

RESTRICTIVE
PURPOSE: To indicate areas where snowmobiling is not permitted.
BACKGROUND COLOR AND LEGEND: Brown with white border and white snowmobile symbol with red diagonal stripe

WARNING

TRAIL INTERSECTION
PURPOSE: To indicate an intersection in the trail.
SIZE: 12"x12"
BACKGROUND COLOR: Yellow
LEGEND: Black 2"x11" vertical and 2"x5¹/₂" diagonal

DANGER
PURPOSE: To indicate an area of danger on the snowmobile trail.
SIZE: 12"x12"
BACKGROUND COLOR: Yellow
LEGEND: Black

INFORMATION

TRAIL BLAZER
PURPOSE: Shows snowmobiler is still on the trail.
SIZE: 5"x7"
BACKGROUND COLOR: Orange with reflective border.

DIRECTIONAL BLAZER
PURPOSE: To indicate changes in trail direction.
SIZE: 9¹/₄"x12"
BACKGROUND COLOR: Orange with black border.
LEGEND: Black 5¹/₄" directional arrow

Ski areas are for skiers. Snowmobile traffic ruins cross-country ski tracks. Respect areas marked with ski signs or blue diamonds. These are cross-country ski trails.

Snowmobile Code of Ethics

1. Do not litter trails or camping areas. Do not pollute streams or lakes.
2. Do not damage living trees, shrubs, or other natural features. Do go out only when there is sufficient snow so that you will not damage the land.
3. Do respect other people's property and rights.
4. Do lend a helping hand to someone in distress.
5. Do make your vehicle available to assist in search and rescue parties.
6. Do not interfere with or harass hikers, skiers, snow-shoers, ice anglers or other winter sports enthusiasts. Do respect their rights to enjoy recreation facilities.
7. Do know and obey all federal, state, and local rules regulating the operation of snowmobiles in areas where you use your vehicle. Do inform public officials when using public lands.
8. Do not harass wildlife. Avoid areas posted for the protection or feeding of wildlife.
9. Do stay on marked trails or marked roads open to snowmobiles. Do not snowmobile where prohibited.

TREAD LIGHTLY!
ON PUBLIC AND PRIVATE LAND

Section II ❄

Directory of Winter Sports Trailheads

This section provides four chapters which include almost 100 percent of the groomed or marked snow trails of California and Nevada.

THE NORTHERN TIER

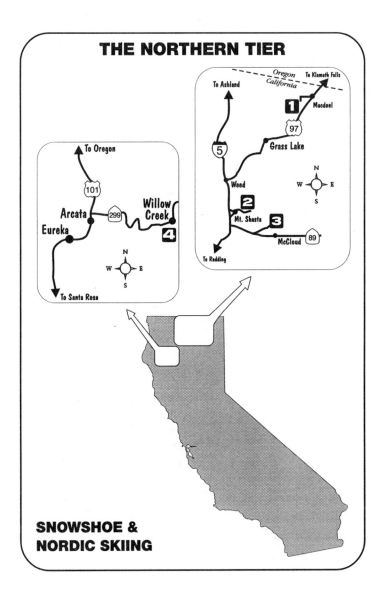

**SNOWSHOE &
NORDIC SKIING**

6 ❄
Snowshoe and Nordic Ski Trailheads

Fifty-two wilderness areas, exclusive of the California Desert, offer non-motorized winter recreation in California and most of these unspoiled tracts have developed trail systems for snowshoers and Nordic skiers. Hardly any other state offers the combination of a great snowpack, excellent snowshoe and ski terrain, heavily-forested areas, glistening alpine scenery and the ease of access which may be found in the "Snowy Range," from the Oregon border to the great California Desert. Even in the desert, several snow-capped peaks invite winter revelers. California is unique in the miles of untrammeled mountain range open to skiers and snowshoers in the Sierra Nevada.

The Northern Tier
❶ JUANITA LAKE, Klamath National Forest
Directions: U.S. 97 to Meiss Lake Road just south of Macdoel. Ten miles west on Meiss Lake Road
Description: Twelve miles of groomed track to Juanita Lake with stunning views of Mt. Shasta and Mt. Mclaughlin.
Fee: No.
Information: Goosenest Ranger District, (916) 398-4391. Snow conditions: (916) 926-2824

❷ EVERITT MEMORIAL HIGHWAY, Shasta/Trinity National Forest

Directions: The Everitt Memorial Highway, A10, ten to twelve miles north and east of Mt. Shasta City.

Description: Three miles of marked, maintained trails: 1) Sand Flat, 2) Overlook Loop, 3) Bunny Flat.

1. Sand Flat: For beginners, 1.3 miles from Upper Sand Flat to Lower Sand Flat on the Sand Flat Road.

2. Overlook Loop: West from Sand Flat for 1 mile. Outstanding views of Mt. Shasta, Mt. Eddy, the Shasta Valley, and the Sacramento River Canyon.

3. Bunny Flat: The trail begins 12 miles up the Everitt Memorial Highway off I-5. Three-quarter-mile track sloping downward toward Sand Flat.

   In addition, unmarked areas to the north and east of Bunny Flat near the Ski Bowl and Castle Lake offer snowshoe/ski opportunities.

Fee: No.

Information: Mt. Shasta Ranger District, (916) 926-4511 weekdays, and (916) 926-3781 weekends.

❸ MT. SHASTA SKI PARK NORDIC CENTER, Commercial

Directions: State Road 89 six miles east of I-5 to Ski Park Highway, north four miles.

Description: 15.5 miles of groomed track for beginners, intermediate, and advanced trekkers.

Fee: Yes.

Information: (916) 926-8610. Snow conditions: (916) 926-8686

❹ HORSE MOUNTAIN, Six Rivers National Forest

Directions: State Road 299, ten miles west of Willow Creek at Berry Summit to FS 1 (Titlow Hill Road) south.
Description: Unmarked tracks over an extensive area.
Fee: No.
Information: Lower Trinity Ranger District, (916) 629-2118

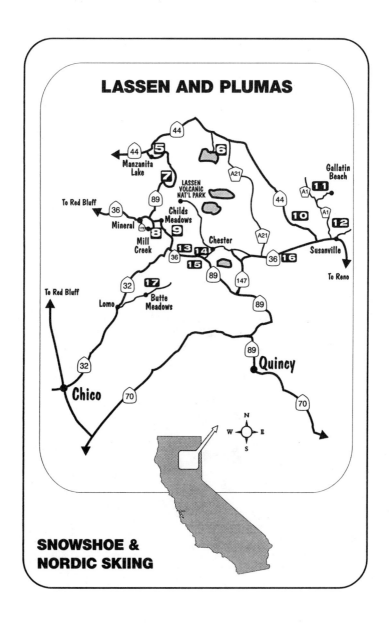

LASSEN AND PLUMAS

SNOWSHOE & NORDIC SKIING

Lassen and Plumas Districts

❺ MANZANITA LAKE, Lassen Volcanic National Park

Directions: Northwest entrance to the park on State Roads 89/44, about six miles east of Viola. One mile south on Road 89 to the end of the plowed area.

Description: A variety of trips on the snowed-over road and Emigrant Trail: six miles roundtrip, 500 foot gain, and Manzanita Creek Trail to Crescent Cliff, ten miles round trip, 1550 foot gain.

Fee: No fee in winter

Information: (916) 595-4444

❻ BUTTE LAKE, Lassen National Forest

Directions: State Road 44 to FS Road 32N21, about 12 miles west of the Bogard Rest Area (47 miles northwest of Susanville on SR 44). South on 32N21.

Description: 14 miles roundtrip to Butte Lake in Lassen National Volcanic Park on Forest Road 32N21.

Fee: No.

Information: Eagle Lake Ranger District, (916) 257-2151

❼ SOUTHWEST CHALET AREA, Lassen Volcanic National Park

Directions: Southwest entrance to the park on State Road 89, ten miles north and east of Mineral. Four miles to the end of the plowed area, Chalet winter sports area.

Description: A dozen possible routes, many difficult as of varying distances: Lake Valley, 6.2 miles; base of Lassen Peak, 7 miles; Kings Creek Meadows, 11.6 miles; Summit Lake, 16.5 miles; Hat Lake 19 miles; Manzanita Lake, 30 miles. Side trips to the Sulfur Works Cutoff, 0.8 miles; Ridge Lakes, 2.5 miles (roundtrip); and Forest Lake, 2.5 miles (loop trip). In addition, unmarked trails

lead to Lassen Peak, 2.5 miles to summit from the road (2000 foot gain); Brokeoff Mountain, 4 miles to the summit from trailhead parking, and may other destinations.
Fee: No fee in winter.
Information: (916) 595-4444

⑧ MILL CREEK, Lassen National Forest
Directions: Closed end of Road 172 (Mill Creek Road), 3.4 miles south of State Road 36.
Description: Three miles along unplowed Road 172 to Mineral Summit. Turnoff to Jones Valley at 2.0 mile post, less than one-half mile south. Alternative: Hole in the Ground Road on south side of Highway 172. Possible cross-country routes of more than ten miles.
Fee: No.
Information: Almanor Ranger District, (916) 258-2141

⑨ WILSON LAKE, Lassen National Forest
Directions: Intersection of Wilson Lake Road and State Road 36, 1.8 miles south of Childs Meadow Resort.
Description: Six miles roundtrip on the snowed-over road to the saddle above Wilson Lake, which provides excellent views of Brokeoff Mountain, Lassen Peak and Mt. Conard. (Five miles to Lake and return.)
Fee: No.
Information: Almanor Ranger District, (916) 258-2141

⑩ HOG FLAT, Lassen National Forest
Directions: State Road 44, 25 miles west of Susanville to Conard Road.
Description: Ten miles of rolling terrain to the Bogard Rest Stop.
Fee: No.
Information: Eagle Lake Ranger District, (916) 257-2151

⓫ EAGLES NEST—EAGLE LAKE, Lassen National Forest

Directions: Eagle Lake Road, A1, 16 miles north of State Road 36. Eagle Lake Road is about three miles west of Susanville.

Description: Snowshoeing all along the perimeter of Eagle Lake.

Fee: No

Information: Eagle Lake Ranger District, (916) 257-2151

⓬ BIZZ JOHNSON NATIONAL RECREATION TRAIL, Lassen National Forest

Directions: Trailheads at Mason Station on County Road A21, four miles north of Westwood; at Goumaz, off State Road 44; Devil's Corral off State Road 36; and in Susanville on Road 36.

Description: Twenty-four and one-half miles of unmarked but easily followed trail along the abandoned Fernley and Lassen Railroad right-of-way. One of the earliest Rails-to-Trails conversions.

Fee: No.

Information: Eagle Lake Ranger District, (916) 257-2151

⓭ STATE ROAD 89, Lassen National Forest

Directions: State Road 89, one mile north of McGowan Road, three miles north of the junction of Roads 36 and 89.

Description: Cross-country along a variety of routes toward the entrance to Lassen National Volcanic Park.

Fee: No.

Information: Almanor Ranger District, (916) 258-2141

⓮ MCGOWAN ROAD, Lassen National Forest

Directions: State Road 89, two miles north of the junction of Roads 36 and 89.

Description: McGowan Road to Viola, 9.2 miles one way. McGowan Lake, 2 miles one-way, and to Plantation ridge, 9 miles roundtrip. The top of the ridge offers great views of Lassen Peak, Brokeoff Mountain and Mt. Conard. Bottle Creek Overlook, 9 miles one way.

Fee: No.

Information: Almanor Ranger District, (916) 258-2141

ⓖ MORGAN SUMMIT TO MINERAL, Lassen National Forest

Directions: State Road 89, two-tenth miles east of the junction of State Roads 36 and 89 to Morgan Summit Snowmobile Park and on to Mineral on Route 36, five miles west of Morgan Summit.

Description: A variety of trails south of State Road 36 which may be combined for lengthy trips:

1. Mineral to Mineral Summit: Junction of Roads 36 and 172 (Mill Creek Road), just south of the gas station. Four miles roundtrip.

2. Conard Grove to Mineral: 1.1 miles east of the Mineral Post Office, one-tenth mile east of the ranger station. Seven miles one way.

3. Conard Grove to Morgan Summit: 1.1 miles east of the Mineral Post Office, one-tenth mile east of the ranger station. Six miles roundtrip. The trip may be shortened by starting at other points along Route 36.

4. Morgan Summit to Mineral—Snowmobile Park at Morgan Summit, west side of State Road 89: Seven miles one way.

5. Morgan summit to the Relay Station: Steady uphill climb for 1.5 miles.

Fee: No.

Information: Almanor Ranger District, (916) 258-2141

🔟 COPPERVALE AREAS, Lassen County

Directions: Thirteen miles west of Susanville off State Road 36.

Description: No marked trails. Cross-country trekking a short distance from the downhill ski slopes.

Fee: No for snowshoe or Nordic skiing.

Information: State Road 36, (916) 256-3866 (adjacent downhill ski resort, (916) 257-9965)

🔟 COLBY CREEK, Lassen National Forest

Directions: State Road 32, 31 miles north of Chico to Butte Meadows Road 91422 (also known as Humboldt Road) at Lomo. Sixteen miles northeast on Butte Meadows Road, 1.5 miles east of Cherry Hill Campground.

Description: Five miles of maintained trails. Adjoins the Jonesville Snowmobile Park, 43 miles of trails.

Fee: No.

Information: Almanor Ranger District, (916) 258-2141 State Road 49

STATE ROAD 49

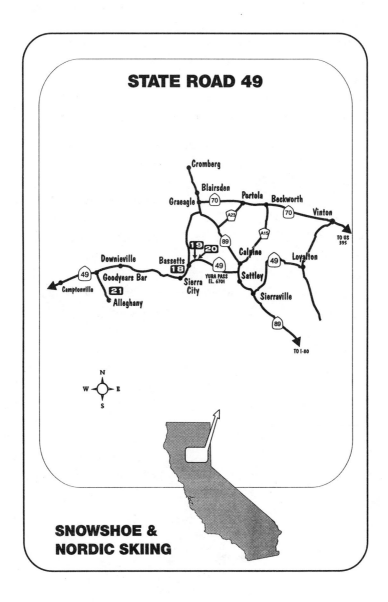

SNOWSHOE & NORDIC SKIING

State Road 49
⓲ GOLD LAKE ROAD, Tahoe National Forest

Directions: Junction of State Road 49 and Gold Lake Road (near Bassett's Station), five miles east of Sierra City.

Description:

1. Gold Lake Road Trail, 17 miles from trailhead to Graeagle. Easy going and excellent views of the Sierra Buttes.
2. Upper Sardine Lake Trail, 7 miles round trip on unmarked Gold Lake and Sardine Lake Roads. A scenic trail to both Upper and Lower Sardine Lakes.
3. Packer Lake Trail, 11 miles round trip on Gold Lake and Packer Lake Roads.

Fee: No.

Information: Sierraville Ranger District, (916) 994-3401 (also Bassett's Station, (916) 862-1297 or (916) 994-3387)

⓳ LUNCH CREEK TRAIL, Tahoe National Forest

Directions: State Road 49 and Lunch Creek Road, one mile west of Yuba Pass.

Description: Trail leads for nine miles north and west from the Yuba Pass, through Beartrap Meadows and beyond, along Lunch Creek.

Fee: Parking at Lunch Creek (limited) No. Parking at Yuba Pass, Yes, Sno-Park

Information: North Yuba Ranger District, (916) 266-3231 (also Bassett's Station; (916) 862-1297 or (916) 994-3387)

⓴ YUBA PASS, Tahoe National Forest

Directions: Highway 49 at Yuba Pass, six miles east of Bassett's Station.

Description: Approximately 100 miles of trail area groomed for snowmobiles, south of Highway 49.

Fee: Yes, Sno-Park
Information: North Yuba Ranger District, (916) 266-3231 (also Bassett's Station; (916) 862-1297 or (916) 994-3387)

㉑ HENNESS PASS ROAD, Tahoe National Forest

Directions: State Road 49 to the Alleghany turnoff, to Pliocene Guard Station at the end of the plowed road (junction of Henness Pass and Pliocene Ridge Roads).
Description: Unmarked area for trips of varying lengths in association with snowmobiles.
Fee: No.
Information: North Yuba Ranger District, (916) 266-3231

I-80 Corridor

㉒ WHEELER LOOP, Tahoe National Forest

Directions: State Road 89 to County Road 450, approximately 15 miles north of Truckee, one mile southeast of Jackson Meadow Road. East on CR450.
Description: Five mile marked loop around the north side of Kyburz Flat east of State Road 89. The flat terrain offers several miles of hikable territory.
Fee: No.
Information: Truckee Ranger District, (916) 587-3558. Avalanche warning report, (916) 587-2158

㉓ SAGEHEN SUMMIT, Tahoe National Forest

Directions: West side of State Road 89 at Sagehen Summit, eight miles north of Truckee.
Description: Unmarked trail of six miles on the creek bottom road. The area offers the possibility of many side trips. The Sagehen Campground is 2.5 miles west of 89.
Fee: No.
Information: Truckee Ranger District, (916) 587-3558. Avalanche warning report, (916) 587-2158

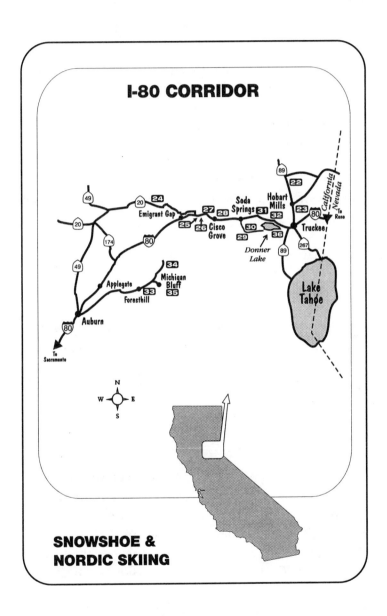

㉔ STEEPHOLLOW, Tahoe National Forest

Directions: On State Road 20, 17 miles east of Nevada City at the Alpha Omega Rest Stop. (Additional parking at turnouts east of the rest stop.)

Description: Eight miles of marked trail, coded by degree of difficulty. A popular cross-country area.

Fee: No.

Information: Nevada City Ranger District, (916) 265-4531 or (916) 265-4538

㉕ YUBA GAP, Nevada County

Directions: I-80, Yuba Gap exit, on the frontage road south of the freeway at the entrance to NACO West Snowflower Campground.

Description: Several miles of easy trail.

Fee: Yes, Sno-Park.

Information: Snowflower Country Store, (916) 389-8241

㉖ EAGLE MOUNTAIN NORDIC, Commercial

Directions: I-80, Yuba Gap exit south of the highway to the end of the plowed road, about one mile.

Description: Ten miles of groomed track, including skating lanes (Nordic ski).

Fee: Yes.

Information: 1-800-391-2254 or (916) 389-2254

㉗ EAGLE LAKES, Tahoe National Forest

Directions: I-80, Eagle Lake exit, north of highway to Indian Spring Campground (Caution: Road may be closed or difficult because of snow conditions.)

Description: Six miles (roundtrip) cross-country along Eagle Lakes/Carlyle Road to Eagle Lakes.

Fee: No.

Information: Nevada City Ranger District, (916) 265-4531

28 RATTLESNAKE, Tahoe National Forest

Directions: I-80, Cisco Grove exit, 79 miles east of Sacramento, north of the freeway to Thousand Trails Campground.

Description: Ten miles of groomed trail along Rattlesnake Road (Fordyce Road) to Magonigal Summit of 1800 feet. An additional three miles of track to Upper Lola Montez Lake.

Fee: Yes, Sno-Park.

Information: Nevada City Ranger District, (916) 265-4531; (also Thousand Trails Campground, (916) 426-3362)

29 ROYAL GORGE, Commercial

Directions: I-80, Soda Springs/Norden exit, two miles south on old Highway 40.

Description: Fifty-three miles, on 77 trails, on 9172 acres, for all level snowshoers and Nordic skiers. Interconnects with the Sugar Bowl Ski Area.

Fee: Yes.

Information: (916) 426-3871

30 CLAIR TAPPAAN LODGE, Sierra Club

Directions: I-80, Soda Springs/Norden exit, three miles south on old Highway 40.

Description: Four miles of varied loop groomed trails to Lytton Lake. Cross-country to Lake Angela and beyond to Lakes Flora and Azalea. Extensive unmarked area for an array of snowplay activities.

Fee: Yes.

Information: (916) 426-3632

31 CASTLE PEAK-DONNER SUMMIT, Tahoe National Forest

Directions: I-80, Castle Peak exit. The Sno-Park is on the frontage road south side of the highway just east of Boreal Lodge.

Description: The trailhead is north of the highway. All snow recreationists must walk about one-quarter mile from the Sno-Park, under I-80 to the starting point. A marked and partially unmarked (but very evident) trail leads in a steady ascent from Castle Valley to Castle Pass, then a slight descent by an unmarked trail to Peter Grubb Hut, a distance of four miles. For longer trips, snowshoers can make their way to Castle or Basin Peaks. The Peter Grubb Hut may be reserved by calling the Sierra Club at Clair Tappaan Lodge, (916) 426-3632. By mail: P.O. Box 36, Norden, CA 95724.
Fee: Yes.
Information: Truckee Ranger District, (916) 587-3558. Avalanche warning: (916) 587-2158

㉜ TAHOE DONNER, Commercial

Directions: I-80, Donner Pass Road exit, east one-half mile on Donner Pass Road to Northwood Boulevard, left (north) five miles to downhill ski area, one mile further to Alder Creek Road. Tahoe Donner cross-country area is about six miles north of I-80.
Description: Thirty-three tracks, including skating lanes, on 11.5 miles of groomed track.
Fee: Yes.
Information: (916) 587-9484

㉝ FORESTHILL DIVIDE, Tahoe National Forest

Directions: I-80, Foresthill Road exit south (road runs northeast) from Auburn, 17 miles to Foresthill.
Description: Twenty-five unmarked miles of untracked, unplowed, Foresthill Road to Robinson Flat.
Fee: No.
Information: Foresthill Ranger District, (916) 367-2224 and (916) 265-4531

❸❹ CHINA WALL STAGING AREA, Tahoe National Forest

Directions: I-80, Foresthill Road exit south (road runs northeast) from Auburn, 17 miles to Foresthill, then 14 miles east of Foresthill on the Foresthill (Divide) Road. A second trailhead is open at Mumford Bar, three miles further along on the Foresthill Road.

Description: Access to several unmarked trails leading to the Mitchell Mine (south), Humbug Ridge (east), and the Mumford Bar.

Fee: No.

Information: Foresthill Ranger District, (916) 367-2224

❸❺ MOSQUITO RIDGE ROAD, Tahoe National Forest

Directions: I-80, Foresthill Road south (road runs northeast) from Auburn, 17 miles to Foresthill to end of plowed Mosquito Ridge Road, east of Foresthill.

Description: Twenty-five unmarked miles of trail from the Interbay turnoff (near Deller Springs) northeast to French Meadows.

Fee: No.

Information: Foresthill Ranger District , (916) 367-2224 and (916) 265-4531

❸❻ DONNER LAKE, Donner Memorial State Park

Directions: I-80, Donner Pass Road exit, south to Emigrant Trail Museum.

Description: Two and one-half miles of gentle, marked track to Donner Lake.

Fee: Yes, Sno-Park.

Information: Museum, (916) 582-7892

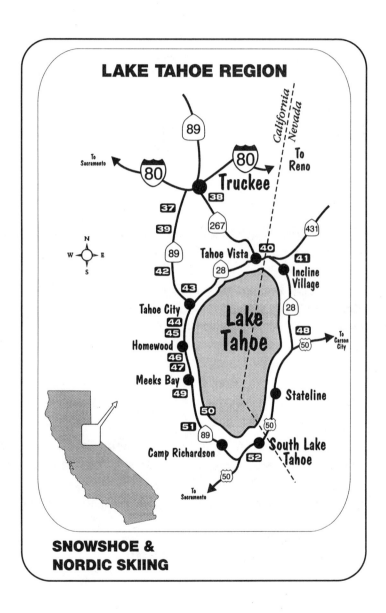

LAKE TAHOE REGION

SNOWSHOE &
NORDIC SKIING

Lake Tahoe Region

③⑦ CABIN CREEK, Tahoe National Forest

Directions: State Road 89, three miles south of I-80, west on Cabin Creek Road for one mile.

Description: Three to six miles of marked trail along old logging roads and the Cabin Creek Road. Some good areas for downhill runs.

Fee: No.

Information: Truckee Ranger District, (916) 587-3558. Avalanche warning, (916) 587-2158

③⑧ NORTHSTAR AT TAHOE CROSS-COUNTRY AND TELEMARK SKI CENTER, Commercial

Directions: On State Road 267, six miles south of Truckee at Northstar.

Description: Ten and one-half miles of groomed trails on 2000 acres, adjacent to the downhill ski area.

Fee: Yes.

Information: (916) 562-1010. Snow phone, (916) 562-1330

③⑨ POLE CREEK TRAIL SYSTEM, Tahoe National Forest

Directions: State Road 89, six miles south of Truckee just south of Little Chief near Bullshead. West side of 89.

Description: Twenty-five miles of unmarked trails on roads and the Pole Creek and Silver Creek drainages.

Fee: Some free parking, some parking at fee.

Information: Truckee Ranger District, (916) 587-3558. Avalanche warning: (916) 587-2158

④⓪ MARTIS LOOKOUT, Tahoe National Forest

Directions: State Road 267, just north of Kings Beach, one-quarter mile north of Brockway Summit.

Description: Up to eight miles of unmarked trails over Martis Lookout Road east of Road 267 to Martis Peak. Great views of Lake Tahoe, Mt. Rose and the Sierra crest.

Fee: No.
Information: Truckee Ranger District, (916) 587-3558.
Avalanche warning: (916) 587-2158

④① DIAMOND PEAK, Commercial

Directions: On Nevada State Road 431, five miles north
of Nevada State Road 28, at Incline Village.
Description: Five and seven-tenths miles of groomed
track and skating lanes (Nordic ski) on 2000 acres.
Fee: Yes.
Information: (702) 832-3249

④② SQUAW CREEK CROSS-COUNTRY SKI CENTER, Commercial

Directions: State Road 89 south from Truckee to Squaw
Valley Road, (five miles north of Tahoe City). West on
Squaw Valley Road 1.5 miles.
Description: Three and one-quarter miles of trail on the
golf course of the Resort At Squaw Creek.
Fee: Yes.
Information: (916) 583-6300, Ext. 6936

④③ LAKEVIEW, Commercial

Directions: State Road 28, 2.5 miles east (north) of
Tahoe City.
Description: Ten and one-half miles of groomed trails on
2000 acres.
Fee: Yes.
Information: (916) 583-9353

④④ PAGE MEADOWS, Lake Tahoe Basin Management Unit

Directions: State Road 89, two miles south of Tahoe
City, west on Fountain Avenue (just north of William
Kent Campground), right on Pine Avenue, left on Tahoe
Park Heights Drive, right on Big Pine Drive, and left on
Silvertip to the end of the plowed road.

Description: No marked trails, but very popular area. Snowshoe the road to Page Meadows.
Fee: No.
Information: (916) 573-2600

45 BLACKWOOD CANYON, Lake Tahoe Basin Management Unit

Directions: State Road 89, three miles south of Tahoe City to Blackwood Canyon Road, across from the Kaspian Picnic Area. West on the road to the Sno-Park.
Description: Two and one-half miles to a play area meadow, and another 4.5 miles (one-way) to Barker pass. The latter section of the trip is strenuous and snowmobiles are allowed.
Fee: Yes, Sno-Park.
Information: (916) 573-2600 or Homewood Hardware, (916) 525-6367

46 MCKINNEY RUBICON ROAD, Lake Tahoe Basin Management Unit

Directions: State Road 89 south from Homewood to McKinney-Rubicon Springs Road, turn west. Take the first left on Bellevue and then the second right on McKinney Road (follow the signs to Miller Lake). Go left on McKinney-Rubicon Springs Road to the end of the plowed road.
Description: Unmarked trail rises 700 feet on a moderate grade to McKinney Lake (two miles) and on to Lily Lake (three miles). More strenuous trips lead to Ellis Peak and Barker Pass.
Fee: No.
Information: (916) 573-2600

47 SUGAR PINE POINT STATE PARK, California Department of Parks and Recreation

Directions: State Road 89, one mile south of Tahoma.

Description: Four marked trails: Red, 3.3 miles; Orange, 1.1 miles; Yellow, 1.8 miles; Blue, 2.1 miles.
Fee: Yes.
Information: (916) 525-7982

④⑧ SPOONER LAKE, Nevada Department of Parks

Directions: At the junction of U.S. 50 and State Road 28 at the Spooner Summit, 11 miles south of Incline Village.
Description: Fifteen miles of groomed trails on 80,000 acres. A short loop around Spooner Lake and a longer trip over unplowed road to Marlette Lake.
Fee: Yes.
Information: (702) 887-8844

④⑨ MEEKS CREEK, Lake Tahoe Basin Management Unit

Directions: State Road 89, one-quarter mile south of the Meeks Bay fire station; one-half mile north of the Meeks Bay Campground.
Description: One and three-quarter miles (one-way) on an old logging road along Meeks Creek. Longer, more strenuous cross country trips to Crag Lake. (Desolation Wilderness permits required for entry to Crag Lake area.)
Fee: No.
Information: (916) 573-2600

⑤⓪ TALLAC HISTORIC SITE, Lake Tahoe Basin Management Unit

Directions: State Road 89 three and one-half miles north of South Lake Tahoe west (south) side of highway at Taylor Creek Sno-Park, near the Visitors Center.
Description: Starting from the Visitors Center, a two mile easy loop around the Kiva Picnic Area.
Fee: No.
Information: (916) 573-2600

51 TAYLOR CREEK, Lake Tahoe Basin Management Unit

Directions: State Road 89, 12.5 miles north of South Lake Tahoe, west (south) side of 89.

Description: Two and one-half miles of level cross country trail from the Sno-park to the north end of Fallen Leaf Lake on the Fallen Leaf Dam Trail. From the dam, a two mile run on the Sawmill Loop Trail. Also from the dam, a two mile Sawmill Loop along the west side of Fallen Leaf Lake.

Fee: Yes, Sno-Park.

Information: (916) 573-2600 (or South Tahoe Shell, (916) 541-2720)

52 ANGORA ROAD, Lake Tahoe Basin Management Unit

Directions: Lake Tahoe Boulevard, 2.5 miles south of the Y on South Lake Tahoe. Turn right on Tahoe Mountain Road and drive to top of the ridge. Turn right at the T intersection on Glenmore Way. Take an immediate left on Dundee Circle and left again on the next street. Park on the street.

Description: Hike on the road and turn left on Forest Service Road 12N14. Two strenuous miles to Angora Lookout (one way), four very strenuous miles to Angora Lake. Wonderful views of the Lake Tahoe Valley and Fallen Leaf Lake.

Fee: No.

Information: (916) 573-2600

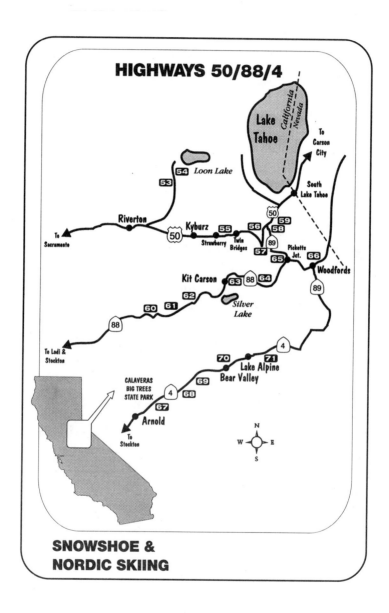

HIGHWAYS 50/88/4

**SNOWSHOE &
NORDIC SKIING**

Highways 50/88/4

53 ROBBS PEAK—ROBBS HUT, Eldorado National Forest

Directions: U.S. 50 to Riverton, 8.5 miles east of Pollock Pines, north on Ice House Road 23 miles to Robbs Peak Road, west on Robbs Peak Road three miles to Robbs Hut. The last three miles may not be passable by car.

Description: Unmarked snowshoe and cross-country ski areas surrounding the hut and its associated lookout tower. The hut, which formerly served as the bunkhouse for the lookout ranger is available for overnight rental. It will accommodate six snowshoers. For information and reservations, call the Eldorado National Forest Information Center, (916) 644-6048.

Fee: No for snowshoers, yes for use of the hut.

Information: Pacific Ranger District, (916) 644-2349

54 LOON LAKE, Eldorado National Forest

Directions: U.S. 50 to Riverton, 8.5 miles east of Pollock Pines, north on the Ice House Road, 30 miles to Loon Lake.

Description: Seven short marked trails (except for the South Shore Trail—unmarked):

1. Zephyr, 0.75 mile
2. Loon Lake Campground, 1.5 miles
3. South Shore, 1.5 miles
4. North Shore, 2.5 miles
5. Berts Lake, 1 mile
6. Chipmunk Bluff, 1 mile
7. Telemark Loop, 1.5 miles.

The Loon Lake Chalet which is located one mile past the Loon Lake Campground, may be visited for overnight use and the loft and warming rooms of the Chalet will accommodate up to 20 snowshoers. Some restrictions apply on

winter weekends when the warming room is open to the public. For information and reservations, call the Eldorado National Forest Information Center, (916) 644-6048.
Fee: No.
Information: Pacific Ranger District, (916) 644-6048

55 STRAWBERRY CANYON NORDIC TRAIL SYSTEM, Eldorado National Forest

Directions: U.S. 50, one-quarter mile west of Strawberry, at 42 mile Recreation Site.
Description: Eleven miles of trails for beginner to intermediate capabilities. Strawberry Ridge Loop, five miles; Cody Creek Loop, 4.5 miles (trail begins at Strawberry Creek Bridge, about three-quarters of one mile from the parking lot); and Station Creek Trail, 1.5 miles of easy track (begins 1.5 miles from parking lot).
Fee: No.
Information: Placerville Ranger District, (916) 644-6048

56 ECHO LAKE, Lake Tahoe Basin Management Unit

Directions: U.S. 50 to Echo Lake Road, six miles east of Strawberry (64 miles east of Placerville). Echo Lakes Road (Johnson Pass Road), north of 50, one-half mile to Sno-Park.
Description: Two and one-half miles to northwest corner of Upper Echo Lake, five miles to Lake Margery, six miles to Lake Aloha. Also three additional loop trails: Becker Loop, 1.5 difficult miles and Firs and Pass Loops, each one-half mile. (Wilderness permit required beyond Echo Lake.)
Fee: Yes, Sno-Park.
Information: (916) 659-0642 or (916) 573-2600

57 ECHO SUMMIT, Lake Tahoe Basin Management Unit

Directions: U.S. 50 to Echo Summit Road, seven miles east of Strawberry (65 miles east of Placerville) Echo Summit Road, south of 50.

Description: Two miles on the Benwood Meadow Loop Trail, an additional mile to Upper Benwood Meadow and cross country beyond, in avalanche territory, on the Pacific Crest Trail. Also, one mile (one way) on the Audrian Lake Trail, starting northwest of the Sno-Park then looping south.

Fee: Yes, Sno-Park.

Information: (916) 573-2600, or (916) 659-0642

58 TROUT CREEK-FOUNTAIN PLACE, Lake Tahoe Basin Management Unit

Directions: From Meyers turn right on Pioneer Trail Drive for three-quarters of one mile to Oneidas Street and turn right to the end of the plowed road.

Description: Two miles along Fountain Place Road to Trout Creek (one way). An additional strenuous two miles to Fountain Place (one way).

Fee: No.

Information: (916) 573-2600

59 LAKE TAHOE WINTER SPORTS CENTER, Commercial

Directions: U.S. 50 one-half mile west of the airport near South Lake Tahoe.

Description: Eleven miles of easy and intermediate trails.

Fee: Yes.

Information: (916) 577-2940

60 LUMBERYARD, Eldorado National Forest

Directions: State Road 88 at the old Lumberyard Ranger Station, 35 miles east of Jackson.

Description: Only one-half mile of easy track parallel to the north side of State Road 88.

Fee: No.

Information: Amador Ranger District, (209) 295-4251, (916) 644-6048

61 PEDDLER HILL, Eldorado National Forest

Directions: State Road 88, at the Old Peddler Hill Ski Area Road, 40 miles east of Jackson, directly across from the Bear River Lake Resort Road.

Description: One mile from 88 northeast along the old road to the Peddler Hill Ski Area. The old ski site offers up and downhill practice.

Fee: No.

Information: Amador Ranger District, (209) 295-4251 and (916) 644-6048

62 LEEK SPRINGS LOOP—IRON MOUNTAIN, Eldorado National Forest

Directions: State Road 88 at the junction with the Mormon Emigrant Trail Road, 45 miles east of Jackson.

Description: Ten miles of marked loop track north of Road 88 along the Emigrant Trail Road, then west to Leek Springs Lookout.

Fee: Yes, Sno-Park

Information: Amador Ranger District, (209) 295-4251 and (916) 644-6048 (or Kit Carson Ski Area, (209) 258-8700)

63 KIRKWOOD, Commercial

Directions: Off State Road 88, just west of Caples Lake.

Description: Thirteen miles of groomed trail on 4200 acres.

Fee: Yes.

Information: (209) 258-7248

64 WINNEMUCCA LAKE LOOP, Eldorado National Forest

Directions: State Road 88 (south side) at Carson Pass, 65 miles east of Jackson. A second parking site, Meiss Meadow, (north side of 88) one-eighth mile west.

Description: Six marked miles of moderately difficult terrain from Carson Pass south to Winnemucca Lake, then northwest to Woods Lake, and finally, along old roads back to Carson Pass.

Fee: Yes, Sno-Park.

Information: Amador Ranger District, (209) 295-4251 and (916) 644-6048

65 GRASS LAKE, Lake Tahoe Basin Management Unit

Directions: State Road 89 south from South Lake Tahoe to Luther Pass, and park in a plowed turn-out.

Description: Three miles (one way) to Hope Valley on unmarked tracks.

Fee: No.

Information: (916) 573-2600

66 HOPE VALLEY CROSS-COUNTRY, Toiyabe National Forest

Directions: State Road 88 at Sorensons, one mile east of the junction of Routes 88 and 89.

Description: Seven thousand acres, 1.5 miles of trail, and eight miles of cross-country runs.

Fee: No, donations accepted.

Information: 1-800-423-9949 or (916) 694-2203

67 CALAVERAS BIG TREES STATE PARK, California Department of Parks and Recreation

Directions: State Road 4 to Calaveras State Park, four miles east of Arnold.

Description: Groomed trails throughout the park.
Fee: Yes, entry.
Information: (209) 795-2334

68 BIG MEADOW, Stanislaus National Forest

Directions: State Road 4 to Big Meadow Picnic Area and immediately east to FS 7N02, one mile east of Liberty Vista, three miles west of Tamarack.
Description: Beginners trail out of the picnic area south of Road 4, and intermediate and advanced trails off FS 7N02, south of Road 4.
Fee: No.
Information: Calaveras Ranger District, (209) 795-1381

69 STATE ROAD 4, Stanislaus National Forest

Directions: State Road 4 to Black Springs, Poison Springs, Cabbage Patch, and Spicer Reservoir, all points east of Calaveras Big Trees and west of Bear Valley.
Description: Many miles of trail, particularly on Black Springs Road, FS 7N23; Poison Springs Road, FS 6N45; Cabbage Patch Road, FS 7N09; and Spicer Reservoir Road, FS 7N11. (See also #68)
Fee: No.
Information: Calaveras Ranger District, (209) 795-1381

70 BEAR VALLEY CROSS-COUNTRY AREA, Commercial

Directions: State Road 4 to Bear Valley Cross Country Area, just west of Bear Valley, thirty-five miles east of Arnold.
Description: Thirty groomed trails over an extensive area.
Fee: Yes.
Information: (209) 753-2834

🌀 LAKE ALPINE, Stanislaus National Forest

Directions: State Road 4 to the end of the plowed road, just past the Bear Valley Ski Area road, 50 miles east of Angels Camp.

Description: Two miles of trail and up to ten miles of cross country tracks, shared with snowmobiles.

1. Eight miles of groomed snowmobile trail from the Sno-Park at Mosquito Lake on snow covered State Road 4.
2. Four miles of loop trail around Lake Alpine.
3. Three miles, round trip, to Pine Marten and Silver Valley Campgrounds.

Fee: Yes, Sno-Park

Information: Calaveras Ranger District, (209) 795-1381

7 ❄
Snowmobile
Trailheads

From the first motor-driven sled in 1927 to the current high speed tractor sleds, snowmobiling has grown to now encompass more than 10,000,000 active participants. California has responded to this growth with the California Department of Parks and Recreation Off-Highway Vehicle Program, known familiarly as the Green Sticker Program. The program has published trail directories, a safety manual, and the *Green Sticker Vehicle,* a biannual newsletter of interest to snowmobilers and off-roaders. More to the point, the program has supported the operations of 72,000 acres of State Vehicular Recreation Areas, and the creation and maintenance of all the formal public snowmobile trailheads, and the grooming of the hundreds of miles of snowmobile track extant in California. At present, the program promotes the California Back Country Discovery Trails efforts (formerly the Motorized Trails Systems) and is a leader in the development of a snowmobile trail to extend from Oregon to the Mexican border. Improvements in the sport are constantly sought by the Green Sticker Program and local snowmobile clubs, most of which are affiliated with the International Snowmobile Council.

THE NORTHERN TIER

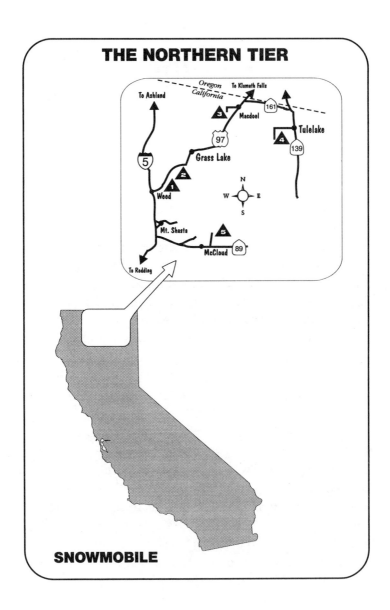

SNOWMOBILE

The Northern Tier

🔺 MEDICINE LAKE LINK, Klamath National Forest

Directions: U.S. 97, five miles northeast of Weed to FS Road 44N01 (Tennant turnoff), ten miles east to parking lot.

Description: Approximately ten miles of loop trails, connecting with Doorknob and Pilgrim Creek Trails.

Fee: No.

Information: Goosenest Ranger District, (916) 398-4391

🔺 DEER MOUNTAIN, Klamath National Forest

Directions: U.S. 97, ten miles northeast of Weed to FS 42N12. or U.S. 19 (Deer Mountain Road), three miles south to park.

Description: Miles of groomed trails radiate from Deer Mountain for access to the north and east sides of Mt. Shasta. The trails link up with three other trail sites.

Fee: No.

Information: Goosenest Ranger District, (916) 398-4391

🔺 FOUR CORNERS, Klamath National Forest

Directions: U.S. 97 one-half mile south of Macdoel to FS Road 15; then 30 miles on FS 15 to park.

Description: Many miles of groomed trails and access to other nearby snow parks.

Fee: No.

Information: Goosenest Ranger District, (916) 398-4391

🔺 DOORKNOB, Modoc National Forest

Directions: State Road 139 to Tule Lake four miles south of the Oregon border, west five miles on East-West Road from Tule Lake, south nine miles on U.S. Road 10 (Hill Road), south six miles on FS Road 49 to park. From the south, take the main road into Lava Beds National Monument off State Road 139, 14 miles west to FS Road 49, six miles to park.

Description: Thirty-one miles of groomed trails, great views of Mt. Shasta.

Fee: No.

Information: Doublehead Ranger District, (916) 667-2246

5 PILGRIM CREEK, Shasta-Trinity National Forest

Directions: State Road 89, three miles east of McCloud to Pilgrim Creek Road. North on Pilgrim Creek Road for eight miles.

Description: One hundred and fifty miles of marked trails. Two trails access the Deer Mountain, Four Corners, and Doorknob Snowmobile Parks of the Klamath and Modoc National Forest. The area is patrolled.

Fee: No.

Information: McCloud Ranger District, (916) 964-2184

Lassen and Plumas Districts

6 ASHPAN, Lassen National Forest

Directions: State Roads 44 and 89, four miles northeast of northern entrance to Lassen Volcanic National Park.

Description: Thirty-nine miles of groomed trails and a warming hut. Highway Loop, 17.8 miles; Butte Loop, 6.6 miles; Grayback Loop, 14.3 miles; and Red Lake Loop, 16.3 miles.

Fee: No.

Information: Hat Creek Ranger District, (916) 336-5521

7 BOGARD REST STOP, Lassen National Forest

Directions: State Road 44 at the Caltrans Rest Stop, 35 miles northwest of Susanville.

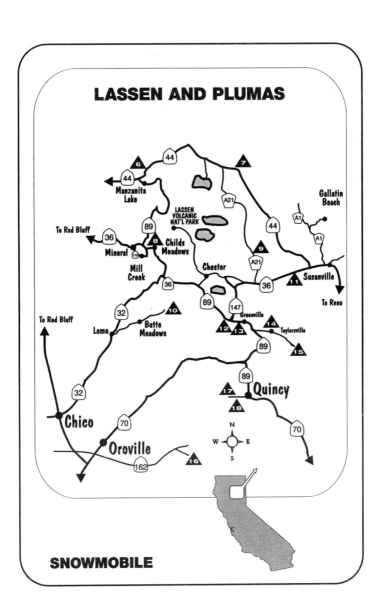

LASSEN AND PLUMAS

SNOWMOBILE

Description: Fifty miles of trails, and connects with Swain Mountain trails.
Fee: No.
Information: Eagle Lake Ranger District, (916) -258-2141

8 MORGAN SUMMIT, Lassen National Forest

Directions: Highway 36, one-half mile east of the southern entrance to Lassen National Volcanic Park, just across from the intersection of State Roads 36 and 89.
Description: Seventy-seven miles of trails and a warming hut.
Fee: No.
Information: Almanor Ranger District, (916) 258-2141

9 SWAIN MOUNTAIN, Lassen National Forest

Directions: County Road A21, about nine miles north of the intersection of A27 and State Road 36.
Description: Forty-seven miles of loop trails around Swain Mountain Experimental Forest to connect with Bogard Rest Stop trailhead.
Fee: No.
Information: Almanor Ranger District, (916) 258-2141

10 JONESVILLE, Lassen National Forest

Directions: State Road 32, 31 miles north of Chico to Butte Meadows Road, 91422, (Humboldt Road) at Lomo. Sixteen miles northeast on Butte Meadows Road to park, 1.5 miles east of Cherry Hill Campground.
Description: Forty-three miles of trails in two major loops to State Road 89 at Humbug Road trailhead.
Fee: No.
Information: Almanor Ranger District, (916) 258-2141

11 FREDONYER SOUTH, Lassen National Forest

Directions: State Road 36, ten miles west of Susanville.

Description: Ten miles of groomed trail, 27 miles of track.

Fee: No.

Information: Eagle Lake Ranger District, (916) 257-2151

▲12 CANYON DAM, Plumas National Forest

Directions: State Road 89 one mile west of the intersection of Roads 89 and 147 at the southern tip of Lake Almanor. Park at the boat launch ramp parking lot on the west side of the dam.

Description: A short track in the Plumas National Forest connects with trails in the Lassen National Forest for many miles of groomed trail.

Fee: No.

Information: Quincy-Greenville Ranger District, (916) 283-0555

▲13 ALMANOR REST AREA, Lassen National Forest

Directions: State Road 89, six miles south of the intersections of Roads 36 and 89.

Description: One hundred miles of trail.

Fee: No.

Information: Almanor Ranger District, (209) 295-4251

▲14 LIGHTS CREEK, Plumas National Forest

Directions: Highway 89, six miles south of Greenville to County Road A22 (FS Road 207) east to Taylorsville (about 5.5 miles). At Taylorsville, North Valley Road, two miles north to Diamond Mountain Road. Northeast on Diamond Mountain Road for five miles or to the end of plowed road.

Description: Several miles of untracked area.

Fee: No.

Information: Quincy-Greenville Ranger District, (916) 283-0555

⚠️15 ANTELOPE LAKE, Plumas National Forest

Directions: State Road 89, six miles south of Greenville to County Road A 22 (U.S. Road 207) east to Taylorsville (about 5.5 miles). At Taylorsville take Genessee Road (also known as Beckwourth and Indian Creek Roads) 25 miles to Antelope Lake or end of the plowed road.

Description: Miles of ungroomed trail on snowed-over Genessee Road.

Fee: No.

Information: Quincy-Greenville Ranger District, (916) 283-0555

⚠️16 FOUR TREES, Plumas National Forest

Directions: State Road 162 east and north of Oroville approximately 15 miles to Oroville Quincy Highway, 20 miles past Elks Retreat to the end of plowed road at Four Corners.

Description: Staging area, some miles beyond the plowed road, connects with the Bucks Lake and Big Creek trails for more than 100 miles of trail.

Fee: No.

Information: Quincy-Greenville Ranger District, (916) 283-0555

⚠️17 BUCKS SUMMIT, Plumas National Forest

Directions: State Road 89 to west end of Quincy, west on Bucks Lake Road (County Road 414) nine miles to park (see # 18).

Description: One hundred miles of groomed trail. Connects with the Four Trees and Big Creek Staging Areas.

Fee: No.

Information: Quincy-Greenville Ranger District, (916) 283-0555

🔺18 BIG CREEK, Plumas National Forest

Directions: State Road 89 to west end of Quincy, west on Bucks Lake Road (County Road 414), seven miles to Big Creek turnoff, 300 yards south on Big Creek Road (see #17).

Description: One hundred miles of groomed trail connecting with Bucks Summit and Four Trees Staging Areas.

Fee: No.

Information: Quincy-Greenville Ranger District , (916) 283-0555

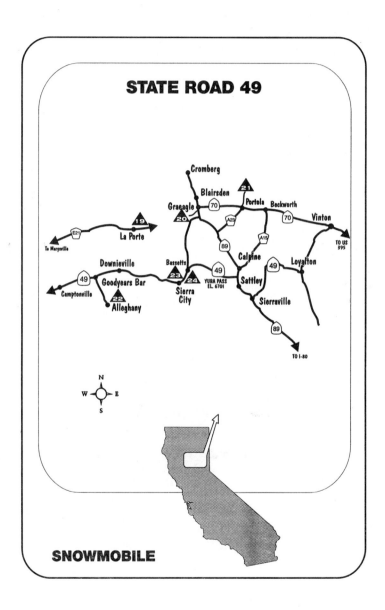

State Road 49

⟨19⟩ LA PORTE, Plumas National Forest

Directions: State Road 20 from Marysville, 12 miles to County Road E 21. Northeast on E 21, 50 miles to east side of La Porte.

Description: Sixty-five miles of groomed trails.

Fee: No.

Information: Oroville-La Porte Ranger District, (916) 534-6500

⟨20⟩ GOLD LAKE, Plumas National Forest

Directions: State Road 89, two miles south of State Road 70, southwest on Gold Lake Road to the end of the plowed area, about five miles.

Description: Seventeen miles of groomed trail on snowed over Gold Lake Road from Highway 49 to Graeagle. Excellent views of the Sierra Buttes. Connects with Yuba Pass, Prosser Hill and other trails for more than 100 miles of trail. See Snowshoe # 17 for Sardine Lake and Packer Lake Trails.

Fee: No.

Information: Mohawk Ranger District, (916) 836-2575

⟨21⟩ LAKE DAVIS, Plumas National Forest

Directions: State Road 70 to Portola, seven miles north on Lake Davis Road.

Description: Eighteen and four-tenth miles, and connects with Smith Peak Loop Trail, three miles.

Fee: No.

Information: Mohawk Ranger District, (916) 836-2575

⟨22⟩ HENNESS PASS ROAD, Tahoe National Forest

Directions: From State Road 49, to Alleghany turnoff, to Pliocene Guard Station at the end of the plowed road (junction of Henness Pass and Pliocene Ridge Roads).

Description: From Henness Pass Road to Jackson Meadow to connect with Yuba Pass Trail. Many possible short loop trails.

Fee: No.

Information: North Yuba Ranger District, (916) 266-3231

⚠23 BASSETT'S STATION, Commercial

Directions: State Road 49 and Gold Lake Road, 20 miles east of Downieville, six miles north of Sierra City.

Description: Connects with Gold Lake Road trails (see #12).

Fee: Yes.

Information: Bassett's, (916) 862-1297

⚠24 YUBA PASS, Tahoe National Forest

Directions: State Road 49 at Yuba pass, south side of highway, six miles east of Bassett's Station.

Description: Seventeen miles of groomed trail north of highway to Gold Lake. Nine miles of trail south of highway. Trails connect with Bassett's Gold Lake, Little Truckee Summit, Prosser and other trails for more than 100 miles of track.

Fee: Yes, Sno-Park.

Information: North Yuba Ranger District, (916) 266-3251 and Bassett's Station, (916) 862-1297

I-80 Corridor

⚠25 RATTLESNAKE, Tahoe National Forest

Directions: I-80, Cisco Grove exit, 79 miles east of Sacramento, north of freeway to Thousand Trails Campground.

Description: Ten miles of groomed trail on Rattlesnake Road (Fordyce Road) to Magonigal Summit, 1800'. Additional three miles of track to Upper Lola Montez Lake.

Fee: Yes, Sno-Park.

Information: Nevada City Ranger District, (916) 265-4531; and Thousand Trails Campground, (916) 426-3362

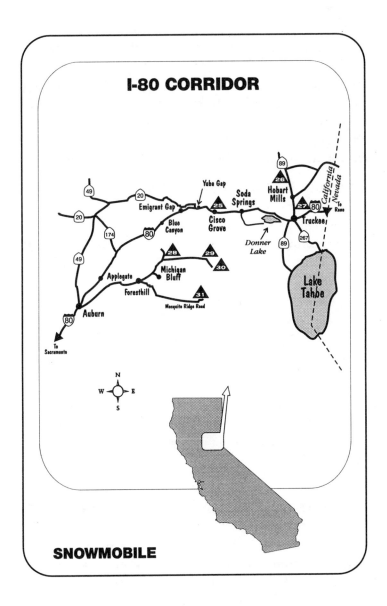

🔺26 LITTLE TRUCKEE SUMMIT, Tahoe National Forest

Directions: I-80 to Truckee, to State Road 89. Seventeen miles north on 89, park at the intersection of 89 and Jackson Meadow Road.

Description: One hundred and ten miles of groomed trails. Connects with Yuba Pass and Prosser Hills (OHV) trails for additional miles of trail.

Fee: No. (Yes at Yuba Pass Trailhead Sno-Park)

Information: Susanville Ranger District, (916) 994-3401

🔺27 PROSSER HILL (OHV), Tahoe National Forest

Directions: I-80 to Truckee to Highway 89. Four miles north on 89 to park.

Description: Twelve miles of marked and groomed trails. Connects with Little Truckee Summit trails for more than 100 miles of trail.

Fee: No.

Information: Truckee Ranger District, (916) 587-3558

🔺28 FORESTHILL DIVIDE, Tahoe National Forest

Directions: I-80, Foresthill Road south (road runs northeast) from Auburn, 15 miles to Foresthill.

Description: Twenty-five unmarked miles of untracked, unplowed, Foresthill Road to Robinson Flat.

Fee: No.

Information: Foresthill Ranger District/Tahoe National Forest, (916) 367-2224

🔺29 CHINA WALL STAGING AREA, Tahoe National Forest

Directions: I-80, Foresthill Road exit south (road runs northeast) from Auburn 15 miles to Foresthill, then 14 miles east of Foresthill on the Foresthill (Divide) Road. A second trailhead is open at Mumford Bar, three miles further along on the Foresthill Road.

Description: Access to several unmarked trails leading to the Mitchell Mine (south), Humbug Ridge (east) and the Mumford Bar.
Fee: No.
Information: Foresthill Ranger District, (916) 367-2224

▲30 CHINA WALL, Tahoe National Forest

Directions: I-80, Foresthill Road exit, south (road runs northeast) one mile north of Auburn. Seventeen miles to Foresthill, then 14 miles east of Foresthill on the Foresthill (Divide) Road. A second trailhead is open at Mumford Bar, three miles further along the Foresthill Road.
Description: Access to several unmarked trails leading to the Mitchell Mine south; Humbry Ridge east; and the Mumford Bar.
Fee: No.
Information: Foresthill Ranger District, (916) 367-2224

▲31 MOSQUITO RIDGE, Tahoe National Forest

Directions: I-80, Foresthill Road exit south (road runs northeast) from Auburn 15 miles to Foresthill to end of plowed Mosquito Ridge Road, east of Foresthill.
Description: Twenty-five unmarked miles from the Interbay turnoff (near Deller Springs) northeast to French Meadows.
Fee: No.
Information: Foresthill Ranger District, (916) 367-2224, Tahoe National Forest, (916) 265-4531

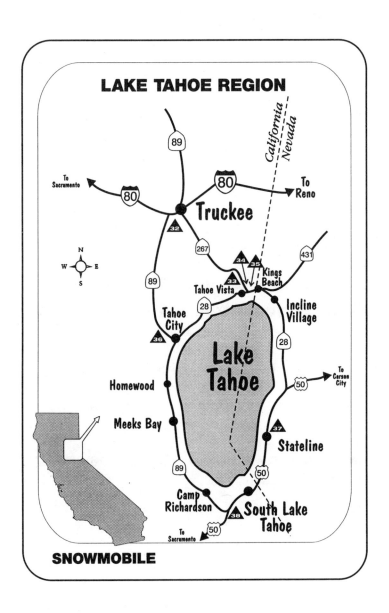

SNOWMOBILE

Lake Tahoe Region

⚠️32 CABIN CREEK, Tahoe National Forest

Directions: State Road 89, three miles south of I-80, right (west) on Cabin Creek Road for one mile.

Description: Three to six miles of marked trail along old logging roads and the Cabin Creek Road. Some good areas for downhill runs.

Fee: No.

Information: Truckee Ranger District, (916) 587-3558, Avalanche warning: (916) 587-2158

⚠️33 NORTH TAHOE REGIONAL PARK, North Tahoe Public Utility District

Directions: State Road 28 two miles west of State Road 267 to Tahoe Vista. Right on National Avenue to Donner Street to park.

Description: One and three-quarters miles of trail (open only as a guided tour) and an oval track.

Fee: No.

Information: (916) 546-4212

⚠️34 HIGH SIERRA SNOWMOBILING, Commercial

Directions: Roads 28 and 267 to Old Brockway Golf Course just west of Kings Beach.

Description: Snowmobile track.

Fee: Yes.

Information: (916) 546-9909

⚠️35 MARTIS LOOKOUT, Tahoe National Forest

Directions: State Road 267, just north of Kings Beach, one-quarter mile north of Brockway Summit.

Description: Up to 8 miles of unmarked trails over Martis Lookout Road east of Road 267 to Martis Peak. Great views of Lake Tahoe, Mt. Rose and the Sierra crest.

Fee: No.

Information: Truckee Ranger District, (916) 587-3558. Avalanche warning: (916) 587-2158

▲ T.C. SNO-MO'S

Directions: Roads 89 and 28 to Tahoe City to Tahoe City Golf Course.
Description: Snowmobile track.
Fee: Yes.
Information: (916) 583-1516

▲ ZEPHYR COVE SNOWMOBILE CENTER, Commercial

Directions: U.S. 50, four miles north of Stateline, Nevada.
Description: Guided snowmobile tours.
Fee: Yes.
Information: (702) 588-3833 or (702) 882-0788

▲ LAKE TAHOE WINTER SPORTS CENTER, Commercial

Directions: U.S. 50, one-half mile west of the airport near South Lake Tahoe on the Lake Tahoe Golf Course.
Description: Guided tours over 22 miles of groomed trail.
Fee: Yes.
Information: (916) 577-2940

Highways 50/88/4

▲ BEAR RIVER, El Dorado National Forest

Directions: State Road 88, 37 miles east of Jackson (about six miles east of Hams Station) to Bear River Road, south for three miles to park.
Description: Twenty-four to 55 miles of trail depending on snow level (average 37 miles), to Salt Springs and Mud Lake. Connects with Iron Mountain and Silver Lake trails.
Fee: No.
Information: Amador Ranger District, (209) 295-4251

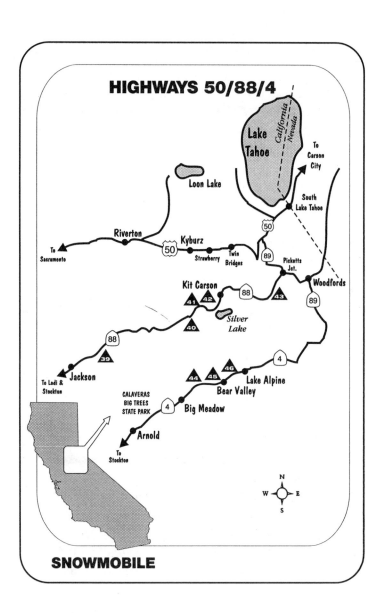

BEAR RIVER LAKE RESORT, Commercial

Directions: State Road 88, 42 miles east of Jackson to Bear River Road, south three miles.
Description: Guided tours over 75 miles of groomed trails.
Fee: Yes.
Information: (209) 295-4868

 IRON MOUNTAIN, El Dorado National Forest

Directions: State Road 88, 45 miles east of Jackson at the junction of 88 and Mormon Emigrant Trail Road.
Description: Twenty-four to 55 miles of groomed trail depending on snow level (average, 37 miles). Leek Springs Lookout and Bear River Reservoir. Connects with Bear River and Silver Lake trails.
Fee: Yes, Sno-Park
Information: Amador Ranger District, (209) 295-4251. Avalanche Report, (916) 587-2158

 SILVER LAKE, El Dorado National Forest

Directions: State Road 88 at Kay's Resort at Silver Lake, north side of the road.
Description: About eight miles of groomed trail to Mud Lake and beyond to Bear River Reservoir to connect with Bear River and Iron Mountain trails.
Fee: No.
Information: Amador Ranger District, (209) 295-4251

 BLUE LAKES—HOPE VALLEY, Toiyabe National Forest

Directions: State Road 88, 6.5 miles east from Carson Pass to Blue Lake Road, three-quarter miles to Hope Valley Campground Road.
Description: Twenty miles of groomed trail and 15 miles of track to Blue Lakes and south to Hermit Valley area west of Ebbetts Pass.
Fee: No.
Information: Carson Ranger District, (702) 882-2766

44 SPICERS RESERVOIR, Stanislaus National Forest

Directions: State Road 4, 23 miles northeast of Arnold (about 2.5 miles east of Big Meadow) to Spicer Road. East on Spicer Road one mile to park.
Description: Several miles of track.
Fee: No.
Information: Calaveras Ranger District, (209) 795-1381

45 STATE ROAD 4, Stanislaus National Forest

Directions: State Road 4 to Black Springs, Poison Springs, Cabbage Patch and Spicer Reservoir Road, all points east of Calaveras Big Trees State Park and west of Bear Valley.
Description: Many miles of trail particularly on Black Springs Road, FS 7N23; Poison Springs Road, FS 6N45; Cabbage Patch Road, FS 7N09; and Spicer Reservoir Road, FS 7N11. State Road 4, groomed for 20 miles from Lake Alpine to Highland Lakes.
Fee: No. (Yes, at Alpine Lake Sno-Park)
Information: Calaveras Ranger District, (209) 795-1381

46 BEAR VALLEY SNOWMOBILE SERVICE, Commercial

Directions: Highway 4 to Bear Valley Village, 25 miles east (north) of Arnold.
Description: Tours on groomed trail to Ebbetts Pass and surrounding areas.
Fee: Yes.
Information: (209) 753-2121

THE NORTHERN TIER

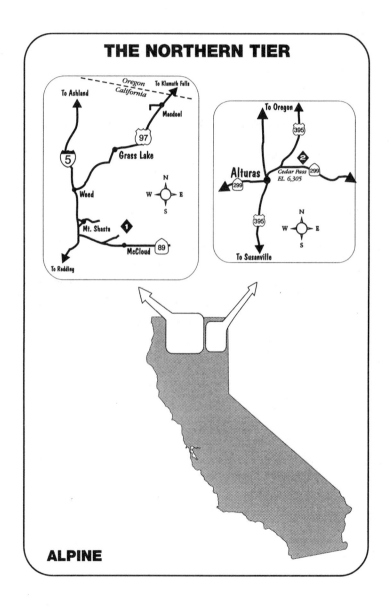

ALPINE

8 ❊
Alpine Ski Resorts

(Note: All downhill ski areas charge fees except for those noted to the contrary.)

The greatest concentration of downhill ski areas in the country is in the Lake Tahoe area. This concentration is not an accidental happenstance, but the product of a great snowpack, between 30 and 40 feet; renowned slopes; sunny, brilliantly clear winter days; stunning alpine scenery; and all-weather access roads. Similar circumstances apply outside the Tahoe area, as dozens of other ski areas throughout the state testify. California has been dubbed "The Downhill Skiers Paradise." Almost all the ski resorts welcome snowboarders, but it is wise to check in advance. Many commercial ski resorts operate in national forests under special use permits from the Forest Service.

The Northern Tier
➊ MOUNT SHASTA SKI PARK, Commercial

Directions: State Road 89 six miles east of I-5 to Ski Park Highway, north four miles.

Description: Twenty-two trails, 3000 acres, three lifts. Peak: 6600′

Fee: Yes.

Information: (916) 926-8610

❷ CEDAR PASS MODOC SKI CLUB, Commercial

Directions: State Road 299, 17 miles east of Alturas.
Description: Five trails, 100 acres, two lifts. Peak: 6400′
Fee: Yes.
Information: (916) 233-2113

Lassen and Plumas Districts
❸ STOVER MOUNTAIN, Stover Mountain Ski Club

Directions: State Road 36, one mile southwest of Chester across from intersection with Road 89.
Description: Four runs, 13 acres, two lifts. Peak: 5500′
Fee: Yes.
Information: (916) 258-4220 (Also Almanor Ranger District, (916) 258-2141

❹ COPPERVALE, Commercial

Directions: State Road 36, nine miles west of Susanville.
Description: Four trails, 80 acres, two lifts. Peak: 6800′
Fee: Yes.
Information: (916) 257-9965

❺ PLUMAS—EUREKA SKI BOWL, Plumas Ski Club

Directions: State Road 70 at Johnsville, 25 miles east of Quincy in Plumas-Eureka State Park.
Description: Six runs, three lifts. Peak: 6150′
Fee: Yes.
Information: (916) 836-2317

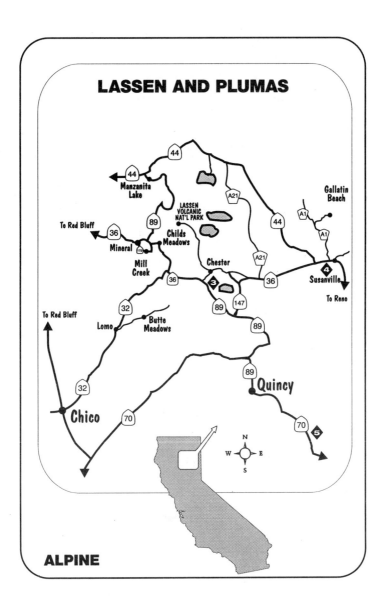

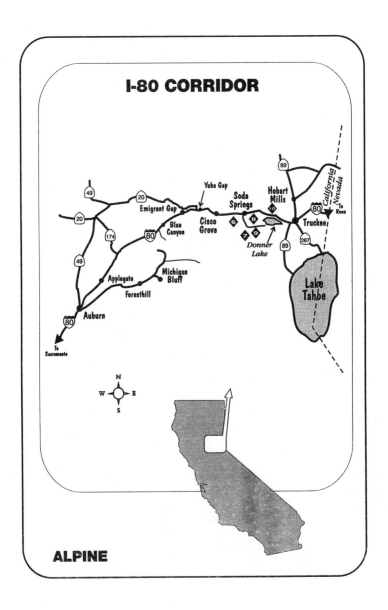

I-80 Corridor

❻ SODA SPRINGS, Commercial

Directions: I-80, Soda Springs exit. East on Old Highway 40 for one mile.

Description: Sixteen trails, 200 acres, two lifts. Peak: 7352'

Fee: Yes.

Information: (916) 426-3666

❼ DONNER SKI RANCH, Commercial

Directions: I-80, Soda Springs exit. East on Old Highway 40 for 3.5 miles.

Description: Forty trails, 360 acres, five lifts. Peak: 7751'

Fee: Yes.

Information: (916) 426-3635

❽ BOREAL, Commercial

Directions: I-80 to Castle Peak exit.

Description: Forty-one trails, nine lifts, 380 acres. Peak: 7800'

Fee: Yes.

Information: (916) 426-3666

❾ SUGAR BOWL, Commercial

Directions: I-80, Soda Springs exit. East on Old Highway 40, for two miles.

Description: Forty-seven trails, 1100 acres, nine lifts. Peak: 8383'

Fee: Yes.

Information: (916) 426-3651

❿ TAHOE DONNER, Commercial

Directions: I-80, Donner Pass Road exit, east one mile to Northwood Boulevard, left (north) five miles.

Description: Eleven runs, 120 acres, two lifts. Peak: 7350'

Fee: Yes.

Information: (916) 587-9444

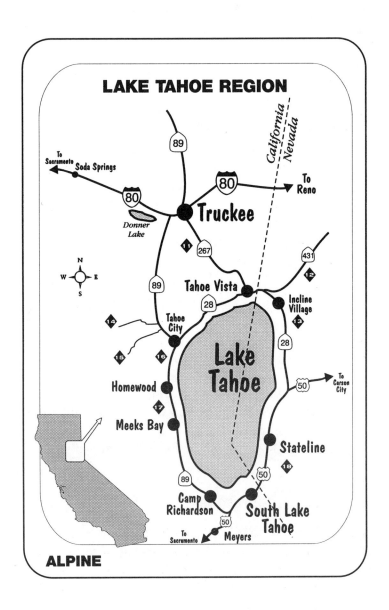

LAKE TAHOE REGION

ALPINE

Lake Tahoe Region

⓫ NORTHSTAR AT TAHOE, Commercial

Directions: State Road 267, seven miles south of Truckee.
Description: Fifty-three trails, 11 lifts. Peak: 8610'
Fee: Yes.
Information: (916) 562-1010

⓬ MOUNT ROSE, Commercial

Directions: Nevada State Road 431, 11 miles northeast of Incline Village, 22 miles southwest of Reno (Road 395 to 431).
Description: Forty-one trails, 900 acres, five lifts. Peak: 9700'
Fee: Yes.
Information: (702) 849-0704

⓭ DIAMOND PEAK, Commercial

Directions: Off Nevada State Road 28, east of Incline Village. North on Country Club Road to Ski Way.
Description: Thirty trails, 655 acres, seven lifts. Peak: 8540'
Fee: Yes.
Information: (702) 832-1177

⓮ SQUAW VALLEY, Commercial

Directions: State Road 89 south from Truckee to Squaw Valley Road (five miles north of Tahoe City). West on Squaw Valley Road three miles.
Description: Four thousand acres served by lifts (8300 acres total), 33 lifts, (five at the peak). Peak: 9050'
Fee: Yes.
Information: (916) 583-6985

⓯ ALPINE MEADOWS, Commercial

Directions: State Road 89 south from Truckee to Alpine Meadows Road (six miles north of Tahoe City). Three miles west on Alpine Meadows Road.

Description: More than 100 trails, 2000 acres, twelve lifts. Peak: 8637′

Fee: Yes.

Information: (916) 583-4232

⑯ GRANLIBAKKEN AT LAKE TAHOE, Commercial

Directions: State Road 89, one mile south of Tahoe City to Granlibakken Road.

Description: One trail, two lifts. Peak: 6610′

Fee: Yes.

Information: (916) 583-9896

⑰ SKI HOMEWOOD, Commercial

Directions: State Road 89, six miles south of Tahoe City.

Description: Fifty-seven trails, 1200 acres, ten lifts. Peak: 7880′

Fee: Yes.

Information: (916) 525-2992

⑱ HEAVENLY, Commercial

Directions: U.S. 50, two miles east of South Lake Tahoe to Stateline.

Description: Sixty-eight trails, 4800 acres, 24 lifts. Peak: 10,040′

Fee: Yes.

Information: (702) 586-7000

Highways 50/88/4

⑲ SIERRA AT TAHOE, Commercial

Directions: U.S. 50, 2.5 miles west of Echo Summit (about 2.5 miles east of Strawberry).

Description: Forty trails, 2000 acres, nine lifts. Peak: 8852′

Fee: Yes.

Information: (916) 659-7475

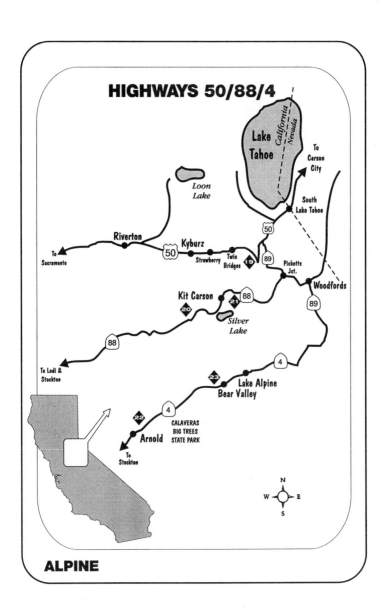

HIGHWAYS 50/88/4

ALPINE

⟨20⟩ KIT CARSON SKI AREA, Commercial

Directions: State Road 88 at the junction with the Mormon Emigrant Trail Road.
Description: Thirty-six trails, 1200 acres, five lifts. Peak: 7800'
Fee: Yes.
Information: (209) 258-8800

⟨21⟩ KIRKWOOD, Commercial

Directions: Off State Road 88, just west of Caples Lake.
Description: Sixty-eight trails, 11 lifts. Peak: 9876'
Fee:
Information: (209) 258-6000

⟨22⟩ COTTAGE SPRINGS, Commercial

Directions: State Road 4, eight miles east of Arnold.
Description: Beginner and learning slopes, two lifts. Peak: 6500'
Fee: Yes.
Information: (209) 795-1401

⟨23⟩ BEAR VALLEY SKI AREA, Commercial

Directions: State Road 4, 92 miles east of Stockton (36 miles east of Arnold).
Description: Sixty trails, 1280 acres, 11 lifts. Peak: 8495'
Fee: Yes.
Information: (209) 753-2301

9 ❄
Snowplay Areas

The term snowplay is practically synonymous with family fun, for snowplay inevitably raises visions of *Saturday Evening Post* covers by Norman Rockwell, sleighbells on Bobtail, wooden toboggans on rural slopes, snowmen with coal eyes and carrot noses, and hot cider indoors after a winter's romp. All of these "long ago and far away" delights are still available, and children are still leading their adult companions into these wonderlands on the slopes of California's snowplay areas.

THE NORTHERN TIER

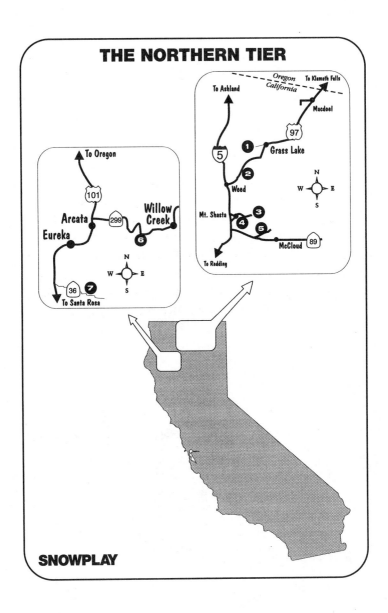

SNOWPLAY

The Northern Tier
❶ FOUR CORNERS, Klamath National Forest
Directions: U.S. 97 to Davis Road, 40 miles north of Weed, 30 miles east of 97 on Davis Road.
Description: Snowplay, snowman construction.
Fee: No.
Information: Goosenest Ranger District, (916) 398-4391

❷ DEER MOUNTAIN, Klamath National Forest
Directions: U.S. 97 to Deer Mountain Road (FS Road 42N12), 15 miles northeast of Weed, three miles east (south) on Deer Mountain Road.
Description: Snowplay, snowman construction.
Fee: No.
Information: Goosenest Ranger District, (916) 398-4391

❸ BUNNY FLAT, Shasta-Trinity National Forest
Directions: The Everitt Memorial Highway, A10, 12 miles north and east of Mt. Shasta City.
Description: Good sledding and snowplay area.
Fee: No.
Information: Mt. Shasta Ranger District, (916) 926-4511 weekdays and (916) 926-3781 weekends.

❹ CASTLE LAKE, Shasta-Trinity National Forest
Directions: I-5 to Mt. Shasta (City) to Barr Road. South on Barr Road three miles to Castle Lake Road.
Description: Ice-skating on Castle Lake for areas cleared of snow.
Fee: No.
Information: Mt. Shasta Ranger District, (916) 926-4511 weekdays and (916) 926-3781 weekends.

❺ SNOWMAN'S HILL, Shasta-Trinity National Forest
Directions: State Road 89, six miles east of I-5.
Description: Good sledding and snowplay.

Fee: No.
Information: Mt. Shasta Ranger District, (916) 926-4511 weekdays and (916) 926-3781 weekends.

➏ HORSE MOUNTAIN, Six Rivers National Forest

Directions: State Road 299, ten miles west of Willow Creek to FS 1 (Titlow Hill Road) south.
Description: Varied snowplay area. No facilities.
Fee: No.
Information: Lower Trinity Ranger District, (916) 629-2118

➐ SOUTH FORK MOUNTAIN, Norse Butte—Six Rivers National Forest

Directions: State Road 36 to Bridgeville, then southeast nine miles to South Fork Mountain Road (FS 4N12).
Description: Varied snowplay area, no facilities.
Fee: No.
Information: Mad River Range District, (707) 574-6233

State Road 49

➑ BASSETT'S STATION, Tahoe National Forest

Directions: State Road 49 at intersection of Gold Lake Road, five miles east of Sierra City.
Description: Snowplay and sledding.
Fee: No.
Information: Sierraville Ranger District, (916) 994-3401 (also Bassett's Station, (916) 862-1297)

➒ YUBA PASS, Tahoe National Forest

Directions: State Road 49 at Yuba Pass, six miles east of Bassett's Station.
Description: Good snowplay, but no sled slope.
Fee: Yes, Sno-Park.
Information: North Yuba Ranger District, (916) 266-3231 (also Bassett's Station, (916) 862-1297)

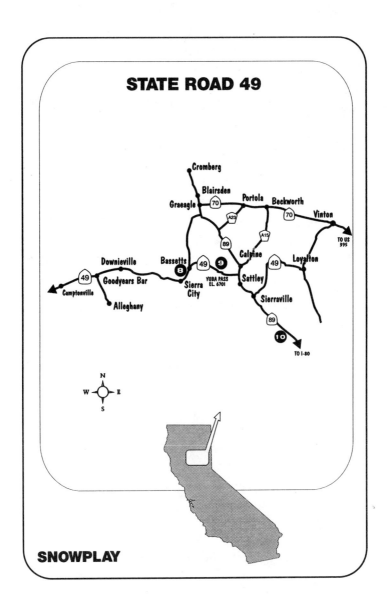

⑩ JACKSON MEADOW, Tahoe National Forest

Directions: State Road 89 and intersection of Jackson Meadow Road sixteen miles north of Truckee.
Description: Good snowplay.
Fee: No.
Information: Truckee Ranger District, (916) 587-2158

I-80 Corridor
⑪ BLUE CANYON, Tahoe National Forest

Directions: I-80 to Blue Canyon exit, south.
Description: Snowplay areas along Blue Canyon Road.
Fee: No.
Information: Nevada City Ranger District, (916) 265-4536

⑫ HIGHWAY 20, Tahoe National Forest

Directions: I-80 to State Road 20 exit, 1.5 miles east of Yuba Gap. West on State Road 20.
Description: Fifteen miles of highway access to several snowplay sites.
Fee: No.
Information: Nevada City Ranger District, (916) 265-4536

⑬ YUBA GAP, Nevada County

Directions: I-80, Yuba Gap exit on the frontage road south of the freeway at the entrance to NACO West Snowflower Campground.
Description: Excellent snowplay with sled slopes.
Fee: Yes, Sno-Park.
Information: Snowflower County Store, (916) 389-8241

⑭ EAGLE MOUNTAIN NORDIC, Commercial

Directions: I-80, Yuba Gap exit. One mile south of freeway on Lake Valley Road to the end of the plowed road.

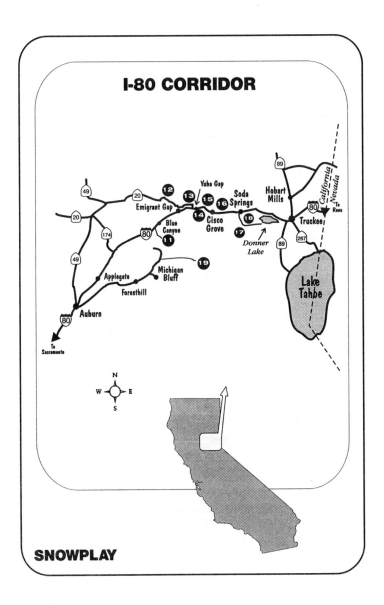

I-80 CORRIDOR

SNOWPLAY

Description: Saucer sliding on groomed hill.
Fee: Yes.
Information: (916) 389-2254

⓯ EAGLE LAKES, Tahoe National Forest
Directions: I-80, Eagle Lake exit north of highway to Indian Spring Campground.
Description: Area beyond the campgrounds provides snowplay with a small sled slope.
Fee: No.
Information: Nevada City Ranger District, (916) 265-4531

⓰ CISCO GROVE, Tahoe National Forest
Directions: I-80, Cisco Grove exit, 79 miles east of Sacramento, north of the freeway to the entrance of Thousand Trails Campground.
Description: Excellent snowplay area with sled slope.
Fee: Yes, Sno-Park.
Information: Nevada City Ranger District, (916) 265-4531

⓱ BOREAL, Commercial
Directions: I-80 to Castle Peak exit.
Description: Restricted area and restricted times.
Fee: Yes.
Information: (916) 426-3666

⓲ DONNER LAKE, Donner Memorial State Park
Directions: I-80, Donner Pass Road exit, south to Emigrant Trail Museum.
Description: Snowplay, no sled slope.
Fee: Yes, Sno-Park
Information: Museum, (916) 582-7892

⑲ CHINA WALL STAGING AREA, Tahoe National Forest

Directions: I-80, Foresthill Road exit south (road runs northeast) from Auburn, 15 miles to Foresthill, then 14 miles east of Foresthill on the Foresthill (Divide) Road.

Description: Excellent area for snowman construction and similar types of snowplay.

Fee: No.

Information: Foresthill Ranger District, (916) 367-2224

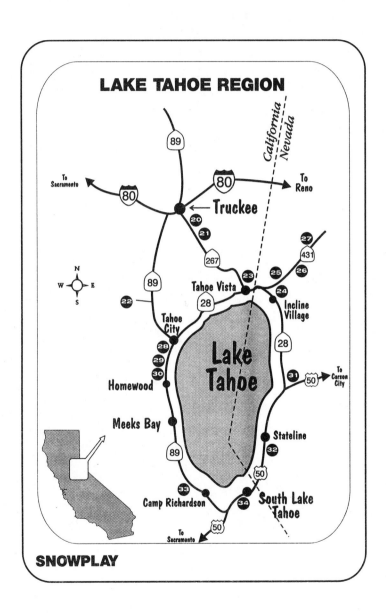

LAKE TAHOE REGION

SNOWPLAY

Lake Tahoe Region

⑳ GLENSHIRE DRIVE, Tahoe National Forest

Directions: State Road 267, five miles south of Truckee to Glenshire Drive.
Description: Varied snowplay.
Fee: No.
Information: Truckee Ranger District, (916) 587-3558

㉑ NORTHSTAR AT TAHOE SLEIGH RIDES, Commercial

Directions: State Road 267, seven miles south of Truckee.
Description: Horse-drawn sleigh rides.
Fee: Yes.
Information: (916) 562-2490, (916) 562-1010

㉒ SQUAW VALLEY, Ice-skating, Commercial

Directions: State Road 89 south from Truckee to Squaw Valley Road (five miles north of Tahoe City), west on Squaw Valley Road three miles.
Description: Open-air Olympic-size ice-skating rink at the top of cable car line.
Fee: Yes.
Information: (916) 583-6985

㉓ NORTH TAHOE REGIONAL PARK, Commercial

Directions: State Road 28 to Tahoe Vista, to the end of National Avenue.
Description: Sleds, toboggans, tubes, saucers (no metal sled runners).
Fee: No.
Information: (916) 546-5043

㉔ INCLINE VILLAGE GOLF RESORT, Commercial

Directions: Nevada State Road 28, 15 miles east of Tahoe City.

Description: Gentle hills off the golf course.
Fee: No.
Information: (707) 832-1143

25 TAHOE MEADOWS, Toiyabe National Forest

Directions: Nevada State Road 431, eight miles north of State Road 28.
Description: Snowplay and sledding (tubes, plastic saucers, and sleds only).
Fee: No.
Information: Carson Ranger District, (702) 882-2766

26 MT. ROSE SUMMIT, Commercial

Directions: Nevada State Road 431, 11 miles northeast of Incline Village, 22 miles southwest of Reno (Road 395 to 431).
Description: Very steep hills for adult sledding.
Fee: Yes.
Information: (702) 849-0704

27 GALENA CREEK PARK, Washoe County

Directions: Nevada State Road 431, 17 miles north of State Road 28.
Description: Snowplay and sledding (tubes, plastic saucers and plastic sleds only).
Fee: No.
Information: (702) 849-2511

28 TAHOE CITY, Lake Tahoe Basin Management Unit

Directions: Highway 89, one-half mile south of Tahoe City just south of Fanny Bridge, east side of the highway.
Description: Gentle sledding slopes, and small family area.
Fee: No.
Information: (916) 573-2600

㉙ GRANLIBAKKEN, Commercial

Directions: State Road 89 one mile south of Tahoe City to Granlibakken Road.
Description: Varied snowplay.
Fee: Yes, Sno-Park.
Information: (916) 583-9896

㉚ BLACKWOOD CANYON, Lake Tahoe Basin Management Area

Directions: State Road 89, 3 miles south of Tahoe City.
Description: Varied snowplay.
Fee: Yes, Sno-Park.
Information: (916) 573-2600

㉛ SPOONER SUMMIT, Commercial

Directions: U.S. 50 at junction with Road 28. Nine miles south of Incline Village.
Description: Steep hills for adult sledding.
Fee: Yes.
Information: (916) 573-2600

㉜ HANSEN'S RESORT, Commercial

Directions: U.S. 50 near Stateline, to 1360 Ski Run Boulevard.
Description: Sledding and tubing hill.
Fee: Yes.
Information: (916) 544-3361

㉝ TAYLOR CREEK, Lake Tahoe Basin Management Unit

Directions: State Road 89, 12.5 miles north of South Lake Tahoe, west (south) side of 89.
Description: Limited snowplay with small sled slope.
Fee: Yes, Sno-Park.
Information: (916) 573-2600 (Or South Tahoe Shell, (916) 541-2720)

㉞ BORGE'S SLEIGH RIDES, Commercial

Directions: U.S. 50 to South Lake Tahoe, next to Caesar's Tahoe.

Description: Thirty-minute narrated rides in a one-horse open sleigh.

Fee: Yes.

Information: (916) 588-2953

Highways 50/88/4

㉟ STRAWBERRY CANYON STABLES, Commercial

Directions: U.S. 50 40 miles east of Placerville, just west of Strawberry Lodge.

Description: Horse-drawn sleigh rides.

Fee: Yes.

Information: (916) 659-7728

㊱ STRAWBERRY LODGE, Commercial

Directions: U.S. 50, 40 miles east of Placerville.

Description: Sledding hills close to the lodge.

Fee: No.

Information: (916) 659-7200

㊲ ECHO SUMMIT, Lake Tahoe Basin Management Unit

Directions: U.S. 50 to Echo Summit Road, seven miles east of Strawberry (65 miles east of Placerville). Echo Summit Road south of Highway 50.

Description: The best snowplay area in the state. Extensive sledding slopes and snowman construction areas.

Fee: Yes, Sno-Park.

Information: (916) 593-2600 or (916) 659-0642

㊳ BEAR RIVER LAKE RESORT, Commercial

Directions: State Road 88 to Bear River Road, 42 miles east of Jackson. South on Bear River Road three miles.

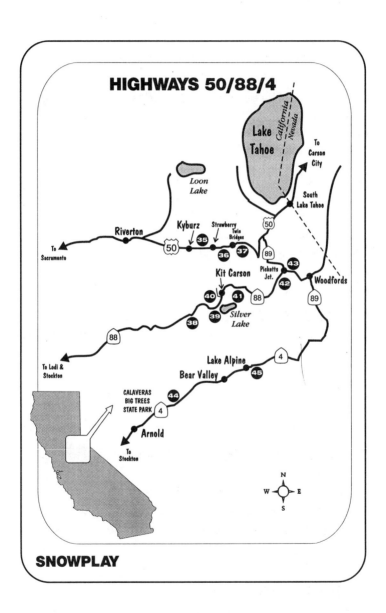

Description: Snowplay.
Fee: Yes.
Information: (209) 295-4868

㊴ KIRKWOOD STABLES, Commercial
Directions: Off State Road 88, just west of Caples Lake.
Description: Horse-drawn sleigh rides around Kirkwood Meadows, 30- to 45-minute rides.
Fee: Yes.
Information: (209) 258-7433

㊵ IRON MOUNTAIN, Eldorado National Forest
Directions: State Road 88 at the junction with the Mormon Emigrant Trail Road, 45 miles east of Jackson.
Description: Good snowplay, no sled slope. Some gentle slopes and bowls good for short saucer runs.
Fee: Yes, Sno-Park.
Information: Amador Ranger District, (209) 295-4251

㊶ CARSON PASS, El Dorado National Forest
Directions: State Road 88 (south side) at Carson Pass, 65 miles east of Jackson. A second parking site at Meiss Meadows (north side of 88) one-eighth mile west.
Description: Limited snowplay, no sled slope.
Fee: Yes, Sno-Park.
Information: Amador Ranger District, (209) 295-4251

㊷ HUSKY EXPRESS—DOG SLED TOURS, Commercial
Directions: State Road 88, 1.5 miles west of junction of Roads 88 and 89 (25 miles south of South Lake Tahoe).
Description: One-hour dog sled tours in the Hope Valley.
Fee: Yes.
Information: (702) 782-3047

㊸ SORENSONS, Commercial
Directions: State Road 88, one mile east of the junction of Routes 88 and 89.

Description: Several sledding slopes for sledding and to-bogganing for guests only.
Fee: Yes.
Information: 1-800-423-9949 or (916) 694-2203

44 STATE ROAD 4, Stanislaus National Forest

Directions: State Road 4, starting at Dorrington, 8.5 miles east of Arnold: 1) Dorrington Fire Station; 2) six miles east, Cottage Springs Play Hill and Cottage Springs Picnic Area; 3) two miles east, Black Springs; 4) 1.5 miles east, Poison Springs; 5) four miles east, Liberty Vista; 6) 1.25 miles east, Cabbage Patch; 7) three miles east, Hells Kitchen and on to Lake Alpine (see #10).

Description:

1) Dorrington, Snowplay and sledding on moderate slope
2) Cottage Springs, Sledding
3) Black Springs, Snowplay
4) Poison Springs, Snowplay and sledding area over unplowed logging road
5) Liberty Vista, Snowplay
6) Cabbage Patch, Snowplay
7) Hells Kitchen, Snowplay

Fee: No.
Information: (916) 583-9896

45 LAKE ALPINE, Stanislaus National Forest

Directions: State Road 4 at the end of the plowed road just past the Bear Valley Ski Area road, 50 miles east of Angels Camp.
Description: Good snowplay, no sled slope.
Fee: Yes, Sno-Park.
Information: Calaveras Ranger District, (209) 795-1381

Section III ❄

Appendix

10 ❄
Leave No Trace

Leave No Trace is a set of ethical principles and associated educational programs designed to protect and conserve outdoor recreation areas, particularly backcountry and wilderness regions. The programs hope to  raise public awareness of the need for such protections. For further information, contact Leave No Trace Inc., P.O. Box 997, Boulder, CO 80306. Phone: 1-800-332-4100, http://www.lnt.org.

Principles of Leave No Trace

PLAN AHEAD AND PREPARE
- Know the regulations and special concerns of the area you'll visit.
- Visit the backcountry in small groups.
- Avoid popular areas during peak-use periods.
- Choose equipment and clothing in subdued colors.
- Repack all food in plastic bags, self-knotted for closure (no twisties or rubber bands). Never take glass into the backcountry.

CAMP AND TRAVEL ON DURABLE SURFACES
On the Trail:
- Stay on designated trails. Walk single file in the middle of the path.

- Stay on the trail on switchbacks. Never use shortcuts.
- When traveling cross-country, choose the most durable surfaces available, such as rock, gravel, dry grasses, or snow. Spread the group. Do not hike single file.
- Use a map and compass to eliminate the need for rock cairns, tree scars, and ribbons. Keep the wilderness wild.
- If you encounter pack animals, step to the downhill side of the trail and speak softly to avoid startling them.
- If you stop to rest, move well off the trail, and sit and keep your pack on a durable surface.

At Camp:
- Choose an established, legal site that will not be damaged by your stay. If possible, use a heavily impacted site. Reject any area showing early signs of impact.
- Restrict activities to areas where vegetation is compacted or absent.
- Keep pollutants out of the water by camping at least 200 feet (about 70 adult steps) from lakes and streams.

PACK IT IN AND PACK IT OUT

- Take everything you bring into the wild back out with you.
- Protect wildlife and your food by storing provisions securely.
- Pick up all spilled foods.

PROPERLY DISPOSE OF WHAT YOU CAN'T PACK OUT

- Deposit human waste in six-by-eight-inch deep catholes at least 200 feet from water, camps, or trails. Cover and disguise the catholes when you're finished.
- Use toilet paper or wipes sparingly; pack them out, or use natural substitutes such as leaves, smooth stones or sticks, snow, etc. Deposit these substitutes in the cathole.

- To wash your dishes, carry the water 200 feet from any stream or lake and scrub the dishes clean (no soap). Rinse with boiling water. Strain the dishwater, deposit the food scraps in the garbage to be carried out, and scatter the gray-water over a wide area. Always minimize the use of soap. To wash your body, handscrub with no soap while swimming or wading. Wash your hands in a basin 200 feet from any water source. Use minimal soap only after toileting or before meal preparation.
- Inspect your campsite for trash and evidence of your stay. Pack out all trash—both yours and others!

LEAVE WHAT YOU FIND

- Treat our natural heritage with respect. Leave plants, rocks, and historical artifacts as you found them.
- Good campsites are found, not made. Do not alter a campsite.
- Let nature's sounds prevail; keep loud voices and noises to a minimum.
- Leave pets at home. If you must take a dog along, keep it under strict control at all times and remove its feces.
- Do not build structures or furniture or dig trenches. Never carry nails, a hammer, an ax or a saw.

MINIMIZE USE AND IMPACT OF FIRE

- Campfires can have a lasting impact on the back-country. Always carry a lightweight stove for cooking, and use a candle lantern instead of a fire whenever possible.
- Where fires are permitted, use established fire rings, fire pans, or mound fires only. Do not scar large rocks or overhangs.
- Gather firewood sticks no larger than an adult's wrist. Gather widely. Do not deplete any area.

- Do not snap branches off live, dead, or downed trees.
- Extinguish campfires totally.
- Remove all unburned trash from the ring for disposal at the trailhead. Burn the wood to a white ash and scatter the cold ashes over a large area well away from any camp.

IN ARID AREAS

- Conserve and use water judiciously.
- Carry your drinking and cooking water if possible.
- Small water holes mean survival for desert creatures. Respect that need. Never bathe or swim in small pools.
- Use small water pockets for drinking only. Dip into the pocket with a clean cup.

11 ❄
Public Agency Directory

USDA Forest Service
Pacific Southwest Region
630 Sansome Street
San Francisco, CA 94111
(415) 705-2874
TTY (415) 705-1098

National Forest Supervisor's and Ranger District Offices

ANGELES NATIONAL FOREST

Supervisor's Office
701 North Santa Anita Avenue
Arcadia, CA 91006
(818) 574-1613

Arroyo Seco Ranger District
Oak Grove Park
Flintridge, CA 91011
(818) 790-1151

Mount Baldy Ranger District
110 North Wabash Avenue
Glendora, CA 91740
(818) 335-1251

Saugus Ranger District
30800 Bouquet Canyon Road
Saugus, CA 91350
(805) 296-9710

Tujunga Ranger District
12371 North Little Tujunga
Canyon Road
San Fernando, CA 91342
(818) 899-1900

Valyermo Ranger District
29835 Valyermo Road
Post Office Box 15
Valyermo, CA 93563
(805) 944-2187

CLEVELAND NATIONAL FOREST

Supervisor's Office
10845 Rancho Bernardo Road
Rancho Bernardo CA 92127-2107
(619) 673-6180
TTY (619) 673-3035

Descanso Ranger District
3348 Alpine Blvd.
Alpine, CA 92001
(619) 445-6235
TTY (619) 445-6235

Palomar Ranger District
1634 Black Canyon Road
Ramona, CA 92065
(619) 788-0250
TTY (619) 788-0250

Trabuco Ranger District
1147 E. Sixth Street
Corona, CA 91720
(909) 276-6390
TTY (714) 736-1811

ELDORADO NATIONAL FOREST

Supervisor's Office
100 Forni Road
Placerville, CA 95667
(916) 622-5061
TTY (916) 626-1552

Amador Ranger District
26280 Silver Drive and Hwy. 88
Star Route 3
Pioneer, CA 95666
(209) 295-4251

Georgetown Ranger District
7600 Wentworth Springs Road
Georgetown, CA 95634
(916) 333-4312

Pacific Ranger District
7887 Highway 50
Pollock Pines, CA 95726

Eldorado Visitor Center
3070 Camino Heights Drive
Camino, CA 95709
(916) 644-6048

Placerville Ranger District
4260 Eight Mile Road
Camino, CA 95667
(916) 644-2324

Placerville Nursery
2375 Fruitridge Road
Camino, CA 95709
(916) 622-9600

INYO NATIONAL FOREST

Supervisor's Office
873 North Main Street
Bishop, CA 93514
(619) 873-2400
TTY (619) 873-2538

Mammoth Ranger District
P.O. Box 148
Mammoth Lakes, CA 93546
(619) 924-5500
TTY (619) 924-5531

Mono Lake Ranger District
P.O. Box 429
Lee Vining, CA 93541
(619) 647-3000
TTY (619) 647-6525

Mount Whitney Ranger District
P.O. Box 8
Lone Pine, CA 93545
(619) 876-6200
TTY (619) 876-5542

White Mountain Ranger District
798 North Main Street
Bishop, CA 93514
(619) 873-250 TTY
(619) 873-2501

KLAMATH NATIONAL FOREST

Supervisor's Office
1312 Fairlane Road
Yreka, CA 96097
(916) 842-6131
TTY (916) 842-5725 or (916) 842-5717

Goosenest Ranger District
37805 Highway 97
Macdoel, CA 96058
(916) 398-4391

Happy Camp Ranger District
P.O. Box 377
Happy Camp, CA 96039
(916) 493-2243

Ukonom Ranger District
P.O. Drawer 410
Orleans, CA 95556
(916) 627-3291

Oak Knoll Ranger District
22541 Highway 96
Klamath River, CA 96050
(916) 465-2241

Salmon River Ranger District
P.O. Box 280
Etna, CA 96027
(916) 467-5757

Scott River Ranger District
11263 South Highway 3
Fort Jones, CA 96032
(916) 468-5351

LAKE TAHOE BASIN MANAGEMENT UNIT

870 Emerald Bay Road, Suite 1
South Lake Tahoe, CA 96150
(916) 573-2600
TTY (916) 541-4036

Tahoe Visitor Center
(916) 573-2674 (summer only)

William Kent Information Station
William Kent Campground
(916) 583-3642 (summer only)

LASSEN NATIONAL FOREST

Supervisor's Office
55 South Sacramento Street
Susanville, CA 96130
(916)257-2151
TTY (916) 257-624

Almanor Ranger District
P.O. Box 767
Chester, CA 96020
(916) 258-2141
TTY (916) 258-2141

Eagle Lake Ranger District
55 South Sacramento Street
Susanville, CA 96130-4565
(916)257-2151
(916) 257-2595 24-hr. No.

Hat Creek Ranger District
P.O. Box 220
Fall River Mills, CA 96028
(916) 336-5521
TTY (916) 258-2141

LOS PADRES NATIONAL FOREST

Supervisor's Office
6144 Calle Real
Goleta, CA 93117
(805) 683-6711
TTY (805) 967-4487

Monterey Ranger District
406 South Mildred
King City, CA 93930
(408) 385-5434
TTY (408) 385-1189

Mount Pinos Ranger District
Star Route, Box 400
Frazier Park, CA 93255
(805) 245-3731

TTY (805) 245-0521

Ojai Ranger District
1190 East Ojai Avenue
Ojai, CA 93023
(805) 646-4348
TTY (805) 646-3866

Santa Lucia Ranger District
1616 North Carlotti Drive
Santa Maria, CA 93454
(805) 925-9538
TTY (805) 925-7388

Santa Barbara Ranger District
Star Route, Los Prietos
Santa Barbara, CA 93105
(805) 967-3481
TTY (805) 967-7337

MENDOCINO NATIONAL FOREST

Supervisor's Office
825 N. Humboldt Street
Willows, CA 95988
(916) 934-3316

Corning Ranger District
22000 Corning Road
P.O. Box 1019
Corning, CA 96021
(916) 824-5196

Covelo Ranger District
78150 Covelo Road
Covelo, CA 95428
(707) 983-6118

Stonyford Ranger District
5080 Ladoga Road
Stonyford, CA 95979
(916) 963-3128

Upper Lake Ranger District
Middlecreek Road
P.O. Box 96
Upper Lake, CA 95485-9500
(707) 275-2361

Genic Resource Center
2741 Cramer Lane
Chico, CA 95926
(916) 895-1176

MODOC NATIONAL FOREST

Supervisor's Office
800 West 12th Street
Alturas, CA 96101
(916) 233-5811

Big Valley Ranger District
P.O. Box 159
Adin, CA 96006
(916) 299-3215

Devil's Garden Ranger District
441 N. Main
Alturas, CA 96101-3457
(916) 233-4611

Doublehead Ranger District
P.O. Box 369
Tulelake, CA 96134
(916) 667-2246

Warner Mountain Ranger District
P.O. Box 369
Cedarville, CA 96104
(916) 279-6116

PLUMAS NATIONAL FOREST

Supervisor's Office
P.O. Box 11500
159 Lawrence Street
Quincy, CA 95971
(916) 283-2050

Greenville Work Center
128 Hot Springs Rd.
Greenville, CA 95947
(916) 284-7126

Challenge Work Center
18050 Mulock Rd.
Challenge, CA 95925
(916) 675-1146

**Milford Ranger District/
Laufman Ranger Station**
Milford, CA 96121
(916) 253-2223

**Beckwourth Ranger District/
Mohawk Ranger Station**
P.O. Box 7
Blairsden, CA 96103
(916) 836-2575

Oroville/La Porte Ranger District
875 Mitchell Avenue
Oroville, CA 95965
(916) 534-6500
TTY (916) 534-6500

Quincy/Greenville Ranger District
39696 Highway 70
Quincy, CA 95971
(916) 283-0555

SAN BERNADINO NATIONAL FOREST

Supervisor's Office
1824 Commercenter Circle
San Bernadino, CA 92408-3430
(909) 383-5588

Arrowhead Ranger District
28104 Highway 18
P.O. Box 7
Rimforest, CA 92378
(909) 337-3437

Big Bear Ranger District
P.O. Box 290
Fawnskin, CA 92333
(909) 866-3437

Cajon Ranger District
Lytle Creek Ranger Station
Star Route, Box 100
Fontana, CA 92336
(909) 887-2576

San Gorgonio Ranger District
Mill Creek Station
34701 Mill Creek Road
Mentone, CA 92359
(909) 794-1123
TTY (714) 389-9133

San Jacinto Ranger District
Idyllwild Ranger Station
54270 Pine Crest Road
Idyllwild, CA 92349
(909) 659-2117

SEQUOIA NATIONAL FOREST

Supervisor's Office
900 West Grand Avenue
Porterville, CA 93257
(209) 784-1500

Greenhorn Ranger District
15701 Highway 178
Bakersfield, CA 93306
(805) 871-2223

Hot Springs Ranger District
Route 4, Box 548
California Hot Springs, CA 93207
(805) 548-6503

Hume Lake Ranger District
35860 East Kings Canyon Road
Dunlap, CA 93621
(209) 338-2251

Cannell Meadow Ranger District
P.O. Box 6
Kernville, CA 93238
(619) 376-3781

Tule River Ranger District
32588 Highway 190
Porterville, CA 93257
(209) 539-2607

Lake Isabella
P.O. Box 3810
Lake Isabella, CA 93240-3810
(619) 379-5646

SHASTA TRINITY NATIONAL FOREST

Supervisor's Office
2400 Washington Avenue
Redding, CA 96001
(916) 246-5222
TTY (916) 246-5313 or (916) 246-5112

Big Bar Ranger District
Star Route 1, Box 10
Big Bar, CA 96010
(916) 623-6106

Hayfork Ranger District
P.O. Box 159
Hayfork, CA 96041
(916) 628-5227

McCloud Ranger District
P.O. Box 1620
McCloud, CA 96057
(916) 964-2184

N.C.S.C.
6101 Airport Road
Redding, CA 96002
(916) 246-5285

Mount Shasta Ranger District
204 West Alma Street
Mount Shasta, CA 96067
(916) 926-4511

Shasta Lake Ranger District
14225 Holiday Drive
Redding, CA 96003
(916) 275-1587

Weaverville Ranger District
P.O. Box 1190
Weaverville, CA 96093
(916) 623-2121

Yolla Bolla Ranger District
Platina, CA 96076
(916) 352-4211

SIERRA NATIONAL FOREST

Supervisor's Office
1600 Tollhouse Road
Clovis, CA 93612
(209) 297-0706
TTY (209) 487-5187 or (209) 487-5155

King's River Ranger District
34849 Maxon Road
Sanger, CA 93567
(209) 855-8321
TTY (209) 855-8321

Minarets Ranger District
57003 Road 225, P.O. Box 10
North Fork, CA 93643
(209) 877-2218

Mariposa Ranger District
43061 Highway 41
Oakhurst, CA 93644
(209) 683-4665
TTY (209) 683-4665

Pineridge Ranger District
P.O. Box 300
Shaver Lake, CA 93664
(209) 841-3311
TTY(209) 841-3311

**Kings River Ranger District/
Dinkey Ranger Station**
Dinkey Route
Shaver Lake, CA 93664
(209) 841-3404 (summer only)

SIX RIVERS NATIONAL FOREST

Supervisor's Office
1330 Bayshore Way
Eureka, CA 95501
(707) 442-1721

Smith River National Recreation Area
P.O. Box 228
Gasquet, CA 95543
(707) 457-3131

Lower Trinity Ranger District
P.O. Box 68
Willow Creek, CA 95573
(916) 629-2118

Mad River Ranger District
Star Route, Box 300
Bridgeville, CA 95526
(707) 574-6233

Orleans Ranger District
Drawer B
Orleans, CA 95556
(916) 627-3291

Salyer Fire Station
Salyer, CA 95563
(916) 629-2114

Zenia Fire Station
General Delivery
Zenia, CA 95495
(707) 923-9669

Humboldt Nursery
4886 Cottage Grove
McKinleyville, CA 95521
(707) 839-3256

STANISLAUS NATIONAL FOREST

Supervisor's Office
19777 Greenley Road
Sonora, CA 95370
(209) 532-3671
TTY (209) 533-0765

Mi-Wok Ranger District
Highway 108 East
P.O. Box 100
Mi-Wok Village, CA 95346
(209) 586-3234

Calaveras Ranger District
Highway 4
P.O. Box 500
Hathaway Pines, CA 95233
(209) 795-1381

Summit Ranger District
#1 Pinecrest Lake Road
Pinecrest, CA 95364
(209) 965-3434

Groveland Ranger District
24545 Highway 120
Star Route
P.O. Box 75G
Groveland, CA 95321
(209) 962-7825

TAHOE NATIONAL FOREST

Supervisor's Office
Highway 49 & Coyote Streets
Nevada City, CA 95959
(916) 265-4531
TTY (916) 478-0310

Nevada City Ranger District
Hwy. 49 & Coyote Streets
Nevada City, CA 95959
(916) 265-4531

Sierraville Ranger District
P.O. Box 95 Highway 89
Sierraville, CA 96126
(916) 994-3401
TTY/Voice (916) 994-3401

Downieville Ranger District
N. Yuba Ranger Station
15924 Highway 29
Camptonville, CA 95922
(916) 478-6253
TTY/Voice (916) 288-3231

Truckee Ranger District
10342 Hwy. 89 North
Truckee, CA 95734
(916) 478-6257
TTY/Voice (916) 587-3558

Foresthill Ranger District
22830 Auburn-Foresthill Road
Foresthill, CA 95631
(916) 478-6254
TTY/Voice (916) 367-2226

Intermediate Region

TOIYABE NATIONAL FOREST

Supervisor's Office
1200 Franklin Ave.
Sparks, NV 89431
(702) 331-6444

Bridgeport Ranger District
Highway 395, P.O. Box 595
Bridgeport, CA 93517
(619) 932-7070

Carson Ranger District
1536 South Carson
Carson City, NV 89701
(702) 882-2766

National Park Service
Ft. Mason Bldg. 201
San Francisco, CA 94123
(415) 556-0561

Yosemite National Park
P.O. Box 577
Yosemite, CA 95389
(209) 372-0264

Lassen National Park
P.O. Box 100
Minerals, CA 96063-0100
(916) 595-4444

Sequoia and King Canyon National Park
P.O. Box 789
Three Rivers, CA 93271
(209) 565-3456

MISTIX
P.O. Box 85705
San Diego, CA 92138-5707
(800) 365-2267

California Department of Parks and Recreation
P.O. Box 942896
Sacramento, CA 94296-0001
(916) 653-6995

Donner Memorial State Park
Donner Pass Road
Truckee, CA 95734
(916) 525-7982

Sugar Pine Point State Park
Highway 89
Tahoma, CA 95733
(916) 582-7892

Nevada Division of State Parks
123 West Nye Lane
Carson City, NV 89710

Spooner Lake Park
P.O. Box 11
Glenbrook, NV 89413
(702) 887-8844

Index ❄

by
Teresa L. Jacobsen

Index by Subject

Index by Trailheads and Geographic Location

Typestyles used:
  Chapter Heads: Sans Black
  Text: New Brunswick,
      New Brunswick Bold
  Page Numbers: Sans Black
  Running Heads: New Brunswick Bold

Printed on recycled paper:
  James River 60 lb. recycled
  white offset